Fast-track You

Fast-track Your Mortgage

Save thousands and live the life you want

Lorraine Graham

ALLEN & UNWIN

First published in 2002

Allen & Unwin
83 Alexander Street
Crows Nest NSW 2065
Australia
Phone: (61 2) 8425 0100
Fax: (61 2) 9906 2218
Email: info@allenandunwin.com
Web: www.allenandunwin.com

National Library of Australia
Cataloguing-in-Publication entry:

Graham, Lorraine, 1954- .
Fast track your mortgage : save thousands and live the life you want.

Includes index.
ISBN 1 86508 805 6.

1. Mortgage loans - Australia - Handbooks, manuals, etc.
2. Finance, Personal - Australia - Handbooks, manuals, etc.
3. Prepayment of debts - Australia - Handbooks, manuals, etc.
4. Saving and investment - Australia - Handbooks, manuals, etc. I. Title.

332.7220994

Set in 11/13 pt Minion by Bookhouse, Sydney
Printed by McPherson's Printing Group

10 9 8 7 6 5 4 3 2 1

Contents

Introduction

For most families, making extra payments on their mortgage is the most effective way they can save money. Most people, however, don't realise just how much they can save by making extra payments or by arranging their mortgage differently.

Competition between banks and other mortgage providers has given us better home loan options and improvements are happening all the time. Most mortgages now offer a redraw facility, allowing you to make extra payments when you have the cash then withdraw the extra money if you need it. This allows you to have your cake and eat it too, making extra payments when you like, yet still having access to the money.

There is more to saving money on your mortgage than just making extra payments when you have a few dollars to spare. This book will show you several ways to save on your mortgage, some of which cost you nothing. I will show you how to work out for yourself the cheapest mortgage option for your situation. I will show you how to calculate how much you will save by fast-tracking your mortgage. For the computer-minded, there are instructions for setting up your own mortgage calculation spreadsheet. The chapter on finding the extra gives heaps of suggestions to save the extra money to pay off your mortgage.

But even better than this, I will show you how to use the thousands of dollars you save to start your own retirement plan and retire wealthy.

The basis of the plan is to put everything you possibly can into paying off your mortgage super fast, then to use the money you were spending on your mortgage payments to build up a range of safe investments to fund your retirement. It sounds simple because it is simple—but it works. Barring major disasters—like employment redundancy, family break-ups or family business failures—it works every time. And if you do have a major disaster, the extra equity you have in your home, and the money you have saved, will help you to get back on your feet more quickly.

You can vary this plan a little if you want to. You may want to move to a larger house and pay off another mortgage before you start to save. This is fine. The method will still work, provided you follow the overall plan.

Here are three examples which will show you how well this method works.

Family A

Family A starts out at age 25 with a mortgage for $100 000, which they pay off in the usual way over 25 years. If the interest rate is 7 per cent, they will pay around $707 per month, plus any fees that their bank charges. Over the 25 years, they will have paid over $112 000 interest on their home loan as well as repaying their original $100 000 principal.

When they have finished paying off the mortgage, they spend their $707 a month on holidays and eating out; they also take out a loan to buy a fast sports car and a boat that they use twice a year. They retire after another 15 years (at age 65) with an old sports car, an old boat (now only used once a year) and a government pension.

Family B

Family B has a similar mortgage, paid off in the usual way over the 25 years. This family pays $112 000 in interest plus the $100 000 principal, the same as Family A. When their mortgage is paid off, they then invest the $707 per month in an investment with a 6 per cent after-tax return for the remaining 15 years. When they retire at age 65 they have around $206 000. This gives them some extra income to supplement their pension—enough for a reasonable lifestyle.

Family C

Family C pays an extra $300 per month off their mortgage, giving them a total monthly payment of $1007. Their mortgage is paid off in less than 13 years. They will have paid around $50 000 in interest on their loan as well as the $100 000 principal. That's $62 000 less than the previous two families. They continue to invest the $1007 at 6 per cent for the remaining 27 years giving them a retirement payment of over $812 000. This will give them a retirement income of well over $50 000 a year. They won't need a government pension.

The extra Family C managed to save over the years has netted them over $600 000 more than Family B and over $800 000 more than Family A. Remember this is using a fairly modest 6 per cent return. If they can manage a return of 8 per cent over this time, the resulting retirement amount is $246 000 for Family B and a whacking $1 157 000 for

Family C. That's over $900 000 more than Family B, and over a million dollars more than Family A.

Family C put the extra $300 per month into their mortgage and savings so they may have done without a few things that Families A and B had, but this book will show you ways of raising the extra without ever missing it. The extra does not all need to be cash, either. We will cover ways to pay your mortgage faster without making extra cash payments.

Inflation will reduce the value of the extra money that Family C has at retirement, but it won't reduce it to nothing. It will still be worth a lot more than the retirement benefit for Family B. You can compensate for inflation by increasing the extra amount that you pay towards your mortgage payment and your investments over the years as your income increases. At the current rate of inflation of around 2–3 per cent, your money will halve in purchasing power over around 30 years. If inflation returns to higher levels, then interest rates will probably go up too, so investment returns will be higher. Inflation cannot be used as an excuse not to save, but you do need to ensure that the after-tax return on your savings and investments is higher than the inflation rate.

What we will cover

This book looks at mortgages and money from different perspectives, from choosing your loan to what to do when you have fully paid for your home. We will cover:

- understanding mortgage types and mortgage terms;
- how mortgage offset accounts work;
- how to work out how much you can afford to spend on a home;

- how to choose the best mortgage options for you;
- how to get started buying a home;
- how to fast-track your mortgage;
- why fast-tracking works;
- how to calculate the benefits of fast-tracking;
- how to get the most benefit from offset accounts;
- why it is better for most families to fast-track their mortgage;
- when it is better to use the money for something else;
- why investment loans are different from home loans;
- managing money to maximise your savings;
- where to find the extra money to fast-track your mortgage;
- what to do when your mortgage is paid off;
- how to choose safe investments for your retirement savings; and
- how to set up a mortgage spreadsheet on a home computer.

I have used a mortgage rate of 7 per cent on a loan of $100 000 over 25 years for the example mortgage in this book. The method works regardless of the prevailing mortgage rate or the amount borrowed. I will show you how to do your own calculations for your rate and amount, and I have included tables for a range of interest rates at the back of this book for people who hate maths. You do not, however, have to do a single calculation or look up any of the tables to fast-track your mortgage. Provided you follow the guidelines, the method will work for you.

I have also assumed you are paid fortnightly for income and money management calculations, and that you pay your mortgage monthly. If your payment interval differs from this, you can easily convert the values. One month is equivalent to 2.17 fortnights or 4.33 weeks. If you want to use the easier conversion of one month to two fortnights or four weeks, this is quite okay. The difference will be small. I have called your normal day-to-day bank account that you access with a card at an automatic teller machine (ATM) a keycard account, and the term bank includes any institution that offers home loans.

As you read through this book, keep in mind our basic plan. You pay off your mortgage as fast as you possibly can, then use the money you were using to pay off your mortgage, including any extra, to build up your retirement savings. There may be faster ways to get rich, but this way never fails.

Be realistic about mortgage pay-off times. To pay off our example $100 000 mortgage in three years, you would need to put in an extra $2373 per month above the normal $707 per month mortgage payment. That's nearly $28 500 per year extra. You may be able to manage this if you have two decent incomes, but for the average single-income family with small children this is totally out of the question. If you plan for ten years, you would need an extra $454 per month which is much more achievable. For 15 years, the extra needed is only $192 per month. Even if you aim for 15 years, you will still be saving over $50 000 in interest over the life of the loan.

Houses cost a lot of money compared to wages because houses cost a lot to build in materials and labour. Borrowing a large sum of money allows you to buy a home when you are young and setting out. If there were no home loans available you would spend years living in rented accommodation, with parents or parents-in-law, or even in a shed, while you saved the money to buy a home. Keep this in mind when you fast-track your mortgage. You will not pay it off by next year, but you can pay it off more quickly and save heaps of interest if you follow the guidelines in this book. The amount you owe will initially seem very large, but no-one is asking you to pay it all back right now. Always think in terms of the money you are saving and the amount you have managed to pay off already, not the frighteningly vast sum you still owe.

There are some calculations in this book. They are all fully explained. If you don't like maths, all calculations are optional. Every single one of them. They are there for people like me who think in maths rather than words and who want to know how to do their own mortgage calculations and how to set up their own computer spreadsheets. There are also tables for people who prefer to look up tables rather than working things out for themselves. At the end of the book is a section on spreadsheet basics and full instructions for writing your own mortgage spreadsheet using Excel. Throughout the book I have included spreadsheet tips for setting up some of the tables yourself. These are for experienced spreadsheet users. There is also a summary list of mortgage equations for people who want to work out the values on a calculator. You will need a scientific or financial calculator for some of them.

If you would like a mortgage spreadsheet, but don't want to write your own, you can download one from my homepage. Here you will also find a current list of mortgage websites and you can download all the spreadsheets and tables from this book. The address is:

www.lainie.com.au

I created my first mortgage spreadsheet when we bought our first home computer in 1986. When I realised the effect of extra payments on reducing our loan balance I started paying off our mortgage as rapidly as I could. I have never looked back. We have paid off loans for the land adjoining ours to extend our garden, and for a weekend property in the south-west of Western Australia. As well as our own home with large garden and our holiday home we now have three rental properties and an ever-increasing portfolio of shares. We have done this on a single income.

I wrote this book for everyone with a mortgage and everyone setting out to buy their first home. I will show you how easy it is to build up your family's assets and retire wealthy. It worked for me, and it will work for you.

Choosing your mortgage 1

The first step in fast-tracking your mortgage is to start with the cheapest possible home loan. This will depend on the options offered by mortgage providers and the amount you are borrowing. Look at the loan options available to you before you start looking for a house. If you already have a home loan, you may be able to restructure it to save you money.

In this chapter we will cover the types of loan commonly available to home buyers, how to work out how much you can borrow, and how to decide which loan type will suit you best.

You and your bank

Before we start, we are going to explode a myth about mortgages. The myth is that the bank is doing you a favour by offering you a mortgage. Gone are the days when you went 'cap in hand' to a bank manager to plead for a loan. Provided you have a good credit rating, a stable job and a reasonable deposit and you are applying to borrow a sensible amount for your income and circumstances, then you have the advantage. You are the customer and you are doing the bank a favour by borrowing money from them. Yes, you did read that correctly. You are doing the bank a favour by borrowing money from them.

The bank doesn't necessarily want you to pay off your loan early, either. You will get a poor credit rating if you default on payments, but it is not in the bank's interest to have you pay off your loan in record time. The aim of the bank is to maximise bank profits, not to save customers money.

Let's look at customers from the bank's point of view.

You borrow $100 000 from the bank at 7 per cent interest. The bank borrows the money they give to you at around 1.5 per cent less than this. The first year you pay the bank nearly $7000 in interest and they get to keep around $1500 of it. They may also charge you a fee of six or eight dollars a month, which you pay without a murmur. This gives the bank a gross yearly amount of around $1600. For this money, their computer takes twelve lots of home loan repayment amounts out of a bank account and sends you a statement at the end of the year. The cost to set up the loan, value the house and sign the mortgage documents is an extra charge to you, usually around $600. The bank may reduce or waive this fee, but they can easily afford to. The next year the interest will be a little bit less than this, as you will have paid off some of the principal, but you will pay over $6000 a year in interest for the first seven years of payments. After seven years on a normal loan, you will still owe over $86 000, and the bank's 1.5 per cent of this is around $1300, so with your $100 in fees the bank will still be gaining nearly $1400 a year even after seven years.

Now, suppose you are a customer with a bank account but not a home loan. You keep an average of around $3000 in a normal keycard account paying 0.1 per cent interest. That's about $3 a year in interest costs to the bank. The bank gets 7 per cent interest lending this money out to someone else, more if they lend it out for personal or business loans rather than home loans. This is about $210 per year, so they make $207. They may charge transaction fees that you resent and try to minimise—say another $100 a year. For this $300 or so they process dozens of transactions, send at least four statements, and run ATMs, EFTPOS terminals and bank branches.

Some customers don't keep anywhere near $3000 in their accounts. Some customers just spend everything they earn, all the time. The bank only makes the $100 a year in transaction fees from these customers, and that in the face of criticism for charging fees at all.

Would you rather be in the lending for home loans business or the running bank accounts business?

Shop around for your loan. Unless you have a ghastly credit rating, ask for discounts, lower fees, free transaction accounts, free credit cards, free or discount home insurance and any other favours you can persuade the bank to give you in exchange for choosing them as your mortgage provider.

Types of loan

There are various options when taking out a home loan. You can have a fixed or variable interest rate, and you can pay principal and interest, or interest only. You can have a budget or no frills option, or you can have a home equity loan. Different banks may have different names for their loan types and loan options.

The main features that vary between loans are:

- whether you pay interest and principal or interest only;

- whether you are on a fixed or variable interest rate;
- whether you have a lower honeymoon rate for the first year;
- whether you can have a redraw, salary or other offset account;
- any set-up and ongoing fees applying to the loan; and
- any perks offered by the bank; for example a transaction-fee-free bank account.

Principal and interest loans

This is the normal sort of loan where you pay off the loan over 25 or 30 years. This is the best choice for most home buyers. These loans can be either fixed or variable rate. Most of what you pay in the first few years is interest, but eventually you pay back the original loan amount.

Interest only loans

These are mainly used for investment home loans, especially for negatively geared rental property, where you can claim any loss you incur on renting the property as a tax deduction, and don't want to put more money than you need to into the investment. (We will cover this situation later in the book, see p 91). Some banks will only give you an interest only loan if you take a fixed rate loan. With interest only fixed rate loans, you are not usually allowed to pay a portion of the original loan amount back before the end of the term. You may be allowed to pay the whole amount back, but there may be a penalty.

Interest only loans can also be used where you need finance for a short time, for example if you have bought a new house before your current house is sold. This is called bridging finance.

Fixed rate loans

With a fixed rate loan the interest is set at the beginning of the loan for the term of the loan, usually from one to five years. You can still take out the loan for 25 or 30 years, as these loans normally just revert to being a variable rate loan at the end of the original fixed term, with no extra charges to pay.

The advantage of this type of loan is that you know exactly what your payments will be for the next few years. If interest rates go up, yours will stay the same. If interest rates go down, however, yours will still stay the same and you could find yourself still paying 8 per cent when everyone else is paying 6 per cent.

If you want to pay this type of loan off early, or refinance it, there may be a penalty, especially if interest rates have come down since you took out the loan. You may not be allowed to make extra payments, either. Check these points if you choose a fixed term loan.

Variable rate loans

For a variable rate loan the interest rate may vary over the life of the loan. This means you can take advantage of lower prevailing interest rates, but your payments will go up if rates go up. If rates go down, keep your payment the same. This is an excellent opportunity to increase the amount you are paying off your mortgage.

Honeymoon rates

Some banks offer a fixed lower rate, called a honeymoon rate, for the first year of the loan. This is usually 0.5 to 1 per cent less than the current variable rate. Remember this honeymoon rate is a fixed rate, and won't change if variable interest rates change during the first year. If interest rates drop during this time, yours will stay the same, so you may lose what you gained. However, if rates go up during the first year of your loan you will gain even more.

Honeymoon rates are normally worth taking. Check that you are allowed to make extra repayments during the fixed rate honeymoon period.

Budget or no frills loans

This is a normal principal and interest home loan with a lower variable interest rate, often around 0.5 per cent lower. The catch is you pay a higher set-up fee, higher ongoing fees, and you may not be allowed to have a redraw account on the loan. (Redraw accounts will be explained shortly.) However, you can usually make extra payments, you only pay the set-up fee once, and you do save a lot in interest. Some banks will allow you to have a redraw account, but with a higher minimum withdrawal amount, and a fee for withdrawal.

The lower fixed honeymoon rate for the first year usually applies to budget loans if you choose to take this feature.

Some banks may not allow you to make extra payments below a certain amount, $1000 for example, on their budget loan. This may make extra repayments less convenient. Ask when you take out your loan whether you can pay back any amount you like whenever you like, or whether they specify a minimum amount.

Combination loans

You may be offered a combination loan, with some of your loan on a variable rate, and some on a fixed rate. If the fixed rate is lower than the variable rate, it may be worth taking the combination loan. There may be restrictions on paying out the fixed rate portion early, so make the variable portion large enough to cover any extra payments you are likely to make during the term of the fixed rate.

Home equity loans

For a home equity loan, you borrow money for another purpose against the equity you already have in your home. This may be money you have already paid off your home loan, or your home may be worth more than you paid for it, so you can borrow more. For instance, if your home is now worth $200 000 and you owe $100 000, you may be able to borrow another $50 000 on your home. You can then use this money to pay for a holiday, to buy a car or to buy shares, or for anything else you want.

You can pay off these loans as for a normal home loan or you can pay interest only. Or you can set the loan up as a revolving line of credit, where you pay interest on the amount of credit you are using at the time, as for a bank overdraft. This way you can pay some of the loan back at any time, then take the money back out again. This type of loan can be used as a monster credit card, with a huge limit and a low interest rate. This could be disastrous for consumer credit addicts, who could reach retiring age with an enormous debt.

Home equity loans usually have a higher interest rate and are not normally used to buy a house initially, but you can set up your loan in this way if you want to. Some banks now set up their standard home loan as an equity loan, and eventually all home loans may be set up like this. If you do choose this option, be careful that you don't get tempted to use the money you borrow for consumer credit, and find yourself getting further into debt instead of paying off the loan.

With a home equity loan, you can usually have your salary paid into the loan just like a bank account, and take out cash when you need it. This effectively gives you the equivalent of a bank account in overdraft. To run a loan like this efficiently, you need to be an excellent money manager, as having your day-to-day money in an account with a huge negative balance makes it difficult to see what you have spent and what you still have available to spend from your pay. It could also be rather depressing to be reminded how much you owe every time you access your bank account balance. However, if you are a good money manager and you rarely or never use up all of your pay, then you can pay off this type of loan quite rapidly without realising you are making any extra repayments at all.

Government subsidised loans

Most state and territory governments have some sort of assistance available to help low-income families buy their own home; for example, Keystart in WA and Homestart in SA.

The two most usual schemes involve help with the initial deposit and buying costs, or structured mortgage payments so you only pay what you can afford, or both. Some states will help with loan payments and deal with the bank for you if you are out of work at some stage and are unable to afford the repayments.

You may be able to put your first home grant (see page 42) towards your deposit, and have your stamp duty reduced. You may be able to have mortgage insurance waived. Mortgage insurance is usually required if you have less than 20 per cent deposit, and protects the lender if you default on your loan payments. We will look at it in more detail shortly.

These schemes will help you to buy a home with little or no deposit. Your income will need to be in a certain range (typically less than $60 000 per year) and the price of the house you are buying will need to be below a set amount, typically around $160 000. However, these limits are reasonably generous.

You may be restricted in your choice of lender, but the rates are usually very competitive on these arranged loans.

For the schemes with structured payments, you pay back a certain percentage of your total income, regardless of whether this amount actually covers the normal payment you would make on the loan. The payment goes up each year with inflation or with your salary, so each year you pay back a little more. If interest rates change, your payment still stays the same. If your payment is insufficient to cover the interest on the loan, then the extra interest is added to the capital, and you may find yourself owing more than you originally borrowed.

This is the sticking point with this type of loan. It allows you to own a home when you might otherwise not be able to afford to, however, you may just be spiralling further and further into debt.

Before you enter into an arrangement where your loan amount is actually increasing, compare the loan repayment with the amount it would cost you to rent a similar home. You may be eligible for a rent subsidy, so include this in your calculation. If it would be cheaper to rent, then it is pointless taking out a loan and owing more and more each year, unless you are really keen to be out of the rent treadmill and into your own place. With this type of loan you do at least have the security of knowing that you will only have to pay a set proportion of your income even if you are unemployed, and by buying your home you will not be subject to rent rises or the whims of landlords.

Offset accounts

With an offset account, you put money into a bank account, and part or all the money is used to reduce the principal of your loan, so you pay less interest, and more of your loan payment each month is going towards paying off the original principal.

In effect, the interest that your money is earning in the offset account at the home loan rate is going towards your payment. This offset interest amount is not classed as income, so you pay no tax on it, and it does not increase your taxable income for family tax benefits, family allowance, Higher Education Contribution Scheme (HECS) repayments or for the superannuation contributions surcharge or the Medicare levy surcharge.

There are three types of offset account, although the names and rules for the account types can vary between banks and between loan types, and they are all only variations on a single theme. Offset account options improve all the time. If you have a home loan, it is worth checking occasionally to find out if any recent changes have made offset accounts more attractive for you.

Redraw accounts

A redraw account allows you to make extra payments off your loan, but still access this money later if you need to. Your bank may call this a repayment redraw facility, rather than a redraw account. Some redraw facilities allow you to redraw every extra dollar you put in, others restrict in some way the total you can withdraw. You may only be able to withdraw payments made in the last five years, for example.

Suppose you had $10 000 saved towards buying a car in a year's time. If you put this money in the redraw account, it will reduce the principal of your loan by $10 000 for the year, saving you around $700 in interest. At the end of the year you can take the money out again, and buy the car. The interest saving is just an offset, you do not have to pay tax on the $700 or declare it as part of your income.

If you had put the $10 000 in the bank in a term deposit at 5 per cent, you would get $500, some of which you would pay in tax. A redraw account is the most efficient way you can save money in a bank, because the effective interest rate is your home loan rate and the interest is tax free.

You are allowed a redraw account on some loan types, but not on others. A redraw account is a very useful thing to have when you are paying off a mortgage. There is usually a minimum amount you are allowed to withdraw. This is normally $2000, but can be up to $5000. There may also be a withdrawal fee of around $50.

Use a redraw account for any money that you won't need for a while. If there is no withdrawal fee, you can afford to have more of your money in the redraw account. If a withdrawal fee is charged, then only use the redraw account for money you are not likely to need for a year or more.

Misa accounts

A Misa account (mortgage interest saver account) is like a redraw account, but the minimum withdrawal amounts are lower and you may not get the whole interest offset. You are normally credited with around 2 per cent of the Misa account balance towards your loan, although some banks will now give you the full offset for your interest rate. The minimum withdrawal amount is lower than for a redraw account (typically $100), and there is usually no withdrawal fee, although there may be a small transaction fee.

There are various names for these accounts, but the features of a Misa account are that the offset is lower than the mortgage rate or there is a small minimum amount you can deposit or withdraw, or both.

Some banks allow you to have a Misa account with an offset lower than the mortgage rate as your normal keycard account. This can be quite useful. Although the offset rate may be low (usually around 2 per cent), it is better than the interest rate for a normal keycard account (around 0.1 per cent from most banks). For example, if you average around $3000 in your keycard account, you will gain around $60 a year by having a Misa account at 2 per cent offset for your main bank account.

If your Misa account has the full offset rate, but there is a minimum withdrawal amount, you may still be able to have your salary paid into the account. Just take out cash in amounts above the minimum, or transfer money to a keycard account. If you are on Internet banking, the transfers are easy. Otherwise you can transfer money at an ATM or by telephoning the bank. Use a credit card for non-cash payments, then pay the balance on the credit card from the Misa account. Check the transaction fees when you open the account, and run your account accordingly. If the transaction fees are high, take out more money less often.

Don't use a Misa account to store money that could be

working much harder in a redraw account if the offset rate is lower for the Misa account.

Salary accounts

A salary account is similar to a Misa account, but always has the full offset, and there is no minimum withdrawal amount. You can usually use a salary account as a normal day-to-day bank account and keep all of your funds in it. Your salary is paid into the account and the balance offsets your home loan at the home loan rate. You may be able to have a keycard on the salary account, or you may just transfer money to a separate keycard account as you need it.

If your loan was for $100 000, and you had $5000 in the account, you would be paying interest on only $95 000. At 7 per cent, this would save you $350 per year. As your account balance builds up, provided you leave your savings amounts in the account, the interest saved will be much higher. This can dramatically reduce the term of the loan and the total interest costs without any extra payments being made.

For a salary account you will gain more offset by paying for everything you can with a credit card. This gives you up to 55 extra days with your money still working for you offsetting your mortgage before you have to pay the credit card balance. Interest on a salary account is usually calculated on the daily balance, so any day you have more money in your account you are making a gain. And the gain is tax free.

The catch is that these accounts are not normally allowed on a budget home loan, so you may be paying an extra 0.5 per cent interest on your loan to have a salary account. This could easily cancel the benefit of the extra offset.

The rules for these accounts vary widely from bank to

bank. Some banks will charge extra transaction fees, and some will not allow you a keycard on the account. Some banks will allow you to have more than one salary account. This would be useful if you like to keep your savings separate from your day-to-day money.

We mentioned home equity loans in the last section and I pointed out that, used as a normal home loan, an equity loan had two disadvantages: the large negative balance that was hard to keep track of, and the temptation to use the loan as a huge credit card. If you have a salary account on a normal home loan, you save exactly the same in interest and pay the loan off just as quickly as you would with a home equity loan without either disadvantage. Unless you particularly need the revolving line of credit advantage of a home equity loan (for example, if you are using equity you already have in your home to borrow money for something else) then set your loan up as a standard home loan with a salary account.

Summary of offset accounts

A summary of the different types of offset accounts is shown in Table 1.1. Your bank may have different names for them, but they usually fall into one of the groups, and this is how I have used the terms in this book.

Costs and perks

Most loans have an initial set-up fee to cover the cost to the bank of setting up the loan, valuing the house and checking your credit rating. The bank may reduce or waive this fee and there are often special loan offers with no set-up fee. In addition to this there are other fees, such as mortgage

Table 1.1 Offset summary

Account type	Usual features
Redraw account	• Full interest rate offset • High minimum withdrawal amount (usually $1000 to $5000) • May have a withdrawal fee of up to $50
Misa account	• Either lower interest offset rate or minimum withdrawal amount (usually around $100) or both • Usually small transaction fees only for withdrawal
Salary account	• Full interest rate offset • No restrictions on deposit or withdrawal amounts • Small transaction fees only for withdrawal

registration. These other fees are not normally rebated by the bank, even if they waive the set-up fee.

Some banks will offer all sorts of perks to encourage you to take your loan with them. The most useful ones are a free credit card and a transaction-fee-free bank account. You may also be offered extra reward points on your credit card or reduced cost (or free) house or life insurance.

It is sometimes difficult to give an exact value to these perks when you are trying to compare loans. If you are currently paying a fee for your credit card, then this can be given a value quite easily. If you are currently paying transaction fees on your bank account, then you can reasonably estimate the saving. If you are offered cheap house insurance, get a quote from another insurance company to compare it to. For life insurance, first decide whether you need it, then get another quote to establish if you are really saving anything. For reward points on a credit card, estimate the redemption value of the points, for example, it may be enough for you to get two $100 shopping vouchers.

Access considerations

It is all very well to choose between all the available loans from banks and other lenders, but if you live outside of a major city, you may need to consider access to banking facilities when you choose your loan provider. A cheaper loan from a particular major bank may not work out cheaper if there is not a branch in your town and you need to drive 50 kilometres to do your banking.

You can overcome this to some extent if your bank has an ATM in your town or if you have access to the Internet. It is possible to be a customer of a bank without ever going into a branch at all. You can transfer money into your loan or redraw account via the Internet or using an ATM. If you don't have access to an ATM, your local store may allow you to take out extra cash using EFTPOS. If you need to bank a cheque, then post it to the nearest branch with a deposit slip. If you need to bank cash on a regular basis, then you are probably stuck. You can deposit money at some ATMs, but usually only the ones outside of a bank branch (which doesn't help much!). As a last resort you could have an account with a local bank as well.

Repayment scheduling

If you are paid weekly or fortnightly, you may be able to make mortgage payments weekly or fortnightly, rather than monthly. This makes managing your money easier. Most banks will allow you to choose the day of the week, fortnight or month that your mortgage is paid. Leave a day or two after your usual payday before the payment is taken out. This allows for delays by your pay department and differences in public holidays between states. If you are paid by cheque, you will need to allow a few days for the cheque to be cleared. Check with your bank on how long they require.

If you change jobs, you may have a different payday. Don't forget to take this into account.

Some lenders and some employers will allow you to have your payment taken directly out of your salary, before you receive it. Again, if you change jobs, you will need to notify the bank.

Most mortgage payments these days are by direct payment from a bank account, so if you want to pay extra you will need to arrange this separately. You may have a deposit book for your loan account, or you may be able to make transfers using Internet banking.

Mortgage insurance

If you borrow more than 80 per cent of the value of your home, you may have to pay mortgage insurance. This insures the bank if you are unable to repay the loan. It does not insure you at all, although you are paying the premium. Mortgage insurance is normally a one-off charge when you take out the loan. You don't pay this amount every year of your loan.

You may be allowed to simply add this amount to the principal of your loan, rather than paying it as a cost, but keep in mind this will increase the proportion you are borrowing.

Mortgage insurance differs slightly between lenders, and can vary from 0.3 per cent of the loan amount, to 1.9 per cent of the loan amount, depending on the lender, the type of loan, the amount of the loan and the proportion borrowed. You will also have to pay stamp duty on the insurance premium, which ranges between 5 per cent to 11 per cent. This can all add up to over $2000 for a loan of $100 000.

Table 1.2 illustrates typical mortgage insurance charges from a major bank. I have used our $100 000 mortgage, and I have added stamp duty at a rate of 10 per cent. Most lenders will not give you a loan for more than 95 per cent of the purchase price.

You may be better off renting a home while you save a decent deposit to avoid paying this extra charge.

Mortgage insurance protects the bank in the event that you default on your loan and they have to sell the house to get back the money you owe them. If the house does not fetch enough to discharge the loan, then the insurance company will pay the bank the difference. The insurance company will then try to get this money back from you. You will have paid hundreds of dollars for insurance that gives you no protection at all.

Table 1.2 Typical mortgage insurance rates

Proportion borrowed %	Insurance rate %	Insurance amount $	Stamp duty at 10%	Total amount $
80–82	0.36	360	36	396
82–84	0.54	540	54	594
84–86	0.68	680	68	748
88–90	0.81	810	81	891
90–92	0.95	950	95	1045
92–94	1.22	1220	122	1342
94–95	1.36	1360	136	1496

Another type of mortgage insurance protects your family in the event that you die or are injured and unable to work. The policy will normally cover the whole amount of the mortgage if you die, so your family will then own the house. Your bank may want you to take out this type of policy. If you have young children, this is probably a good idea. However, if you already have a life insurance policy for this amount of money, either privately or through your super fund, you may not need an extra one.

Some policies will cover your mortgage payments if you are out of work or sick, but this type of insurance is usually expensive. If you do become unemployed and are having difficulty with mortgage payments, most banks will allow you to add some of the interest you owe to the capital, and resume payments when you find a job. Banks are normally quite flexible in this regard. If you have made extra payments, the bank will usually allow you to stop making payments for a while until the extra is used up. The important thing here is to let the bank know there are problems before the payment is due. If they try to take the payment out of your account and the money simply isn't there, then you may have to pay extra fees.

How much can you borrow

Talk to a bank about how much you can borrow on your income. There are normally set rules about the proportion of your total income that you can use to pay off the loan. This is usually around one-third of your gross income. They will also look at your other loan commitments, such as car repayments and credit card balances, and regular payments on these loans will be subtracted from this amount. If you want to borrow the maximum possible, then pay off all credit card balances before you apply, and settle for an older car that you can afford to buy with cash, rather than buying a brand new car on hire purchase.

Don't simply accept the amount the bank recommends you borrow. The bank works on average family spending and the repayment amount may be too much for your lifestyle. Work out for yourself whether you can really afford this level of repayments. Be conservative.

Working this out

Keep track of everything you spend for a few weeks, apart from rent and fixed costs like insurance and power (we deal with these separately). Keep receipts for all purchases. Remember to include costs for which you don't normally get a receipt, like petrol, parking or train fares. Add up all the amounts and work out an average living cost per month.

If you are paying off your car, work out the amount per month that you pay. If you fully own your car, then work out an amount you need to set aside each month towards replacing your car in the future. If you buy a car costing around $24 000 after trade-in every ten years, then this would be around $200 per month. If you replace your car with a new one every five years, increase this to around $300. If your family has two cars, allow two amounts. If you always buy second-hand cars and keep them for a long time, then $100 per month may be sufficient.

To calculate this more accurately yourself, think about when you would be likely to replace your current car and how much the replacement is likely to cost you, allowing for some resale value on your own car. Work out the number of months to go, and divide the cost by this. Then add around $20 a month to allow for price rises.

Next add up all the fixed costs you pay during the year, excluding rent. This will include health insurance, power and gas, car registration, car insurance, telephone, Internet connection costs, union fees and club subscriptions. Add to this the costs you will pay as homeowner that you don't pay now, including house insurance, water charges and council rates. If you don't know what these will cost, ask someone you know who owns their home for an estimate.

Divide the total of all the existing and likely fixed costs by 12 to give an average per month. Add this to the living cost you worked out previously, and add the amount you worked out for car payment or next car. Add about $200 a month to this figure to allow for emergency costs like major car repairs, computer upgrades and failed washing machines. Add another $100 a month to allow for interest rate rises.

Now work out what you are paid per month. If you are paid fortnightly, multiply your take-home pay by 2.17. For weekly, multiply by 4.33. If both partners work, include the second income. Include any Family Allowance and Family Tax Benefit you receive.

Subtract the total amount you calculated for costs from the amount of your take-home pay. This is the maximum realistic amount you can use to pay off your loan. Remember this does not allow you much scope for making extra payments, or for saving money for your retirement or for long-term goals.

We will talk a bit more about allocating your income for various purposes in Chapter 4, Managing Money. At the moment we only need reasonable cost estimates. Table 1.3 is an example.

When you have worked out an amount you can easily pay

Table 1.3 Amount available for mortgage repayment

Cost	Amt per month
Living costs	1300
Fixed costs	400
Car payments or car saving	300
Emergency costs	200
Allowance for rate rises	100
Total costs per month	**2300**
Pay per month (both partners)	3500
Less costs from above	−2300
Available for mortgage	**1200**

off your loan, you can work out how much you can borrow for this repayment amount. You can estimate this for yourself using the payment amounts in Table 1.4, or ask your bank to work it out for you.

You may be charged a monthly loan fee, usually around $6 to $10. You can add this to the repayment amount from the table to give your total payment per month, or just ignore it as not being significant.

A larger table, with the payments calculated for smaller interest rate intervals, is included in the Tables section at the end of the book.

Using the repayment table

Suppose you can manage $1200 per month, and the current interest rate is 7 per cent. To work out what you could borrow, divide the $1200 by $707 (the payment per month from

Table 1.4 Payments per month for a loan of $100 000 at various interest rates

AMOUNT = 100 000
YEARS = 25

Rate %	Payment $
4.0	528
4.5	556
5.0	585
5.5	614
6.0	644
6.5	675
7.0	707
7.5	739
8.0	772
8.5	805
9.0	839
9.5	874
10.0	909
10.5	944
11.0	980
11.5	1016
12.0	1053
12.5	1090

Table 1.4 for $100 000 at 7 per cent) and multiply by the $100 000. This would give you around $170 000.

$$(1200/707) \times 100\,000 = 169\,731$$

Use the normal home loan rate for this calculation, not the lower honeymoon rate that you pay for the first year. You

Spreadsheet tip

To set up this table yourself on an Excel spreadsheet or to calculate the value for your own mortgage, the formula you need is:

$$\text{Payment} = \frac{P \times r \times (1 + r)^n}{(1 + r)^n - 1}$$

P is the Principal

r is the interest rate per period, in this case the yearly rate divided by 12

n is the number of payments. For a 25-year loan, this would be 300.

The function for Excel is

= PMT (Interest rate per mth, No of mths, – present value, future value, type)

The present value is the amount you owe. You will need to put a minus in front of this amount. The future value is zero because you will have paid the loan off. The type is zero because the payment is made at the end of each month.

may prefer to make this calculation using a rate 0.5 to 1 per cent above the current rate, so you allow more for interest rises in the future. If you use the honeymoon rate you could find yourself in trouble when the real rate kicks in.

Remember that this calculation represents the most you can currently afford to borrow. You are not obliged to borrow this much. If you borrow a lower amount you are less likely to be financially stressed if interest rates go up, if you lose your job, or if you live on one income for a while when your children are small.

Contact your bank and ask how much they will lend on your income. It may be different from your own calculation. If the amount you think you can afford is less than the amount the bank recommends that you borrow, then use your figures. Otherwise use the bank's recommended amount.

If you think you can manage more than the bank recommends, and you have personal accounting figures to prove it, then by all means give the bank the details and apply for more. But remember banks set these limits because borrowers have got themselves into financial hot water by committing to loans that they could not afford to pay off. The banks have legal and moral obligations to avoid borrowers over-committing themselves.

Thirty-year loans

You may be able to borrow a bit more if you have a 30-year loan instead of a 25-year loan. Taking out our standard loan ($100 000 at 7 per cent) over 30 years instead of 25 years will lower your payment by only $41 per month, and, if paid over the full 30 years, will cost $27 475 in extra interest. If you need to borrow everything you possibly can for a particular home that you would otherwise not be able to afford, you could take the 30-year term. Otherwise keep to 25 years.

Keep in mind, though, that if you are intending to fast-track your mortgage right from the beginning, then the original loan term is not all that important. A 30-year loan will give you more scope for things going wrong. If you go through a patch where you can't afford any extra, the amount you need each month for the standard payment will be lower.

Choosing your loan

The choice available in loans can be rather daunting, and banks tend to offer products that differ slightly in detail. Ask around at all the banks for details of what they offer. Most places will post you the information if you telephone them. Don't be talked into having a mobile banker call on you at this stage. You want to look at the options yourself, without being hassled. There are websites on the Internet that compare the features of various home loans. Do a search on 'home loan' for Australian sites.

As well as banks, building societies and credit unions, there are now specialist non-bank home loan providers. Home loans are all these organisations deal in, and they have mobile representatives who come to your home. This saves on office infrastructure, and they have no bank branches to run. They get the money they lend to you by selling mortgage bonds to large investors, such as superannuation funds. Most of the interest you pay on your loan is paid to the investor, with the home loan organisation taking the rest to cover their costs and profits. I will call all of these lending institutions banks throughout this book.

For most people, the ideal is a budget variable rate home loan with a redraw account, a free credit card, a bank account free of transaction fees, a zero loan set-up fee, and a honeymoon rate for the first year. You may not get all this with a budget loan, but there is no harm in asking. A salary account would also be nice, but you are unlikely to get this with a budget loan. If you are a good money manager, then a standard loan with a salary account may suit you better. If you go through a non-bank lender, you may not be offered free banking, although some of these institutions do provide free bank accounts for their home loan customers.

I will show you how to work out for yourself the options that will work best for you.

Shop around

Get the best deal you can when getting a home loan. Look at all the mortgage providers rather than just going to the bank where you've been a customer since you first started banking in primary school. Even half a per cent difference in interest rates can make a $100 000 loan $500 a year cheaper. This is worth changing banks for.

To work this out, just multiply the difference in the interest rates by the total amount of the loan. To do this on your calculator, type in:

100 000 × 0.5%

You may be able to get an interest rate discount of 0.5 per cent or so at some banks if you have some types of bank account or credit card, or are a member of some professional institutions or associations or trade unions. Ask your bank about this. This will give you a loan with the budget loan rate and the standard loan perks.

Most banks will give you a free credit card if you have a home loan with them. This is normally the type of credit card with up to 55 days interest free. You may have a free credit card anyway, through a trade union, professional association or university. These are usually called affinity cards.

You may also be offered a transaction-fee-free account for

having a home loan. This may be worth several hundred dollars a year if you make a lot of transactions.

Banks and mortgage providers have excellent websites with details of the loans they offer. As Internet sites are changing all the time, the best way to find these is to do an Internet search of Australian sites using 'mortgage' or 'home loan' as a keyword. I have included a list of some useful sites at the end of this book.

There are some sites that compare the rates and conditions between banks. This is the ultimate in hassle-free choosing from home. There is usually a table comparing conditions and prices that you can print off and take with you when you visit the bank. You may need to get more details of the loan and account conditions from the bank, however. For example, a salary account from one bank may have different conditions to another bank, and this may not show up on an Internet table comparing loans.

Don't expect the choice of loan provider or loan type to be clear cut. A loan may be cheaper in some aspects but not in others. The interest may be higher on one loan than another but the perks may be worth more to you. I will show you on page 31 how to work out the benefits of loans with different conditions. Your bank or mortgage broker may also be able to advise you on the best loan for you.

Rates and conditions are changing all the time, so check the details are still the same when you actually apply for the loan.

Checklist

Here is a list of what to ask when you go to a bank to discuss a loan. Write all the details down. Don't rely on memory. If you can get the information in writing from the bank, so much the better.

- What is the interest rate for the type of loan? Is it fixed or variable? Is there a lower honeymoon rate for the first year? Is a budget loan with a lower interest rate available? Are you eligible for a rate discount?
- What is the loan set-up fee, and can this be reduced or waived?
- What are the fees for registering the mortgage, valuing the property, and mortgage stamp duty?
- What are the ongoing monthly fees?
- Can you make extra payments whenever you like and is there a minimum repayment amount? If you bank on the Internet, ask if you can have your loan account linked and make extra payments when you like.
- Is there a penalty for early repayment of your loan?
- Will you need to pay mortgage insurance? If so, what will it cost? This is normally only required if you are borrowing more than 80 per cent of the purchase price, but some banks charge it on all loans above a certain amount.
- Will your loan entitle you to a free credit card or a keycard account free of transaction fees?
- Does the bank offer any other perks, such as cut price home insurance?
- Can you have a redraw facility? If so, what is the minimum withdrawal amount and is there a fee for withdrawal? Can you withdraw all previous extra payments or are there limits on this?
- Can you have a Misa account? If so, what is the offset rate and the minimum deposit and withdrawal amount?

- Can you have a salary account with a full offset? If so, what are the details relating to this? For example, can you have keycard access, and are you allowed more than one salary account?

Fixed or variable

The first choice you need to make is whether to take a fixed interest rate for the first one to five years of your loan. If you compare the rates and the fixed interest loan has a lower rate, don't immediately think the choice is clear cut and jump in and choose the fixed rate. Interest rates can change, and they can change quite rapidly. If fixed interest rates are lower than variable rates, then naturally the bank is expecting rates to go down in the future. If fixed rates are higher than the current variable rate, then the banks are expecting rates to rise.

Taking a fixed rate because the rates are lower is unlikely on average to be worthwhile, because the risk factor is already built into the rate.

The basic variable mortgage rates are influenced by lending rates set by the Reserve Bank and vary according to the state of the economy. Rate rises and falls are not easy to predict, even for banks, and the banks will tell you they don't actually set their fixed rates according to what they think will happen, but in response to moves in term deposit and bond rates. These in turn are set by market forces and what savvy investors are willing to invest their money for.

If fixed rates are lower, then it may be worth taking a combination loan with part of your loan at the fixed rate. But do be careful with terms of more than two or three years if you are not allowed to pay out the fixed portion early. You may pay your loan off faster than you think.

Fixed one-year honeymoon rates are usually worth taking, because they are often at a fairly hefty discount to the normal variable rate, and small changes to interest rates are unlikely to cover the difference. Most banks will allow you to make extra payments in the honeymoon period as for a normal variable rate loan, but check this with your bank.

One of the advantages of a fixed interest rate is that you know what your repayments will be for several years ahead. Rate rises will not affect your repayment amount. The main disadvantage is that you may not be allowed to make extra repayments on your loan.

If you intend from the beginning to pay your loan off as rapidly as possible, then a variable rate loan is more flexible and much easier to keep track of. Most people choose a variable rate, but you don't have to follow the crowd if the idea of a stable long-term repayment level appeals to you, or if you believe for some reason that rates are on the rise.

Comparing loans

So now you have all the loan details. How do you work out which loan is best for you?

We are going to calculate the costs of two variable rate loans over the first three years to see which loan would be cheaper over that time. Three years gets us over the effect of the set-up fees and the honeymoon rate. As loan products and interest rates can change quite quickly, we don't want to go much further than this. If we have not saved on our loan type by the end of three years, we may never save.

The first loan is a budget loan from a bank and the second is a standard loan from the same bank. You can compare as many loans as you like using this method. Just set up a list or

Table 1.5 Comparing loans

Loan type	Budget	Standard
Interest year one	6000	6000
Interest year two	6500	7000
Interest year three	6500	7000
Loan set-up fee	600	0
Loan ongoing fees 3 years	360	180
Account fees	390	0
Value of offset account	0	-840
Total cost for three years	**20 350**	**19 340**

a computer spreadsheet with one column for each loan you want to compare and one extra column for the row headings. Follow the example in Table 1.5 as you work out all the costs. If the maths here is beyond you, your bank or mortgage broker will be able to advise you on your best options.

For the example, I have used an original amount of $100 000, a variable rate of 7 per cent for the standard loan and 6.5 per cent for the budget loan. The honeymoon rate is 6 per cent for both loan types.

Calculate the first year's interest using the honeymoon rate if this is offered for your loan type. Otherwise use the normal rate for your loan type. Calculate this for the original loan amount by multiplying the loan amount by the percentage rate for the first year. The amount you have paid off the principal by the end of the first year will not make much difference.

The second row gives the interest in the second year. Again calculate this using the original loan amount. This is accurate enough for this calculation. The interest for year three is the same amount as year two.

Now put in the set-up fee. I have used $600 for the budget loan and zero for the standard loan. These are just example amounts. Set-up fees vary between banks and may be waived in some circumstances.

Next are the loan transaction fees that you pay per month. Work out the amount you would pay over the three years. I have used $10 per month for the budget loan, and $5 per month for the standard loan. That gives $360 and $180.

Next put in the value of any credit card fee you currently pay and any bank transaction fees if these are not included as a perk on your loan. Multiply these amounts by three for the three years. I have assumed here that the budget loan does not give you a free card or account and the standard loan does. I have used $30 per year for the credit card, and $100 per year for the transaction fees. This gives $130 per year, and $390 for the three years. Use your last year's bank statements to work out your own transaction fees, but keep in mind that the fees may have been reduced for money you had in an account that is now going out as a deposit. These fees are money you pay with a budget loan but don't with a standard loan, so put this in as a cost on the budget loan.

Now we need to take offset accounts into consideration. We will assume our budget loan allows a redraw account with a minimum withdrawal amount of $5000 and a $50 withdrawal fee, while our standard loan offers a salary account. For our salary account, all of our money is offsetting the home loan. For the redraw account, only the money we don't need for a while is in the redraw.

This reserve money that we don't need for a while is earning the same offset whether it is in a redraw account or a salary account, so we can disregard it. The money we are concerned with here is the day-to-day amount that we are not able to put into the redraw on the budget loan because we need frequent access to it. You need to estimate how much on average you would keep in your day-to-day account, and how much you would put into the redraw. This will vary with your lifestyle, with how frequently you are paid, and even with the time of year. You will need a larger day-to-day amount if you are paid monthly rather than weekly, and you will need more when large bills are due for payment and at Christmas. If you are paid weekly or fortnightly, you will need about a month's pay as an average amount, if you are paid monthly, six weeks' pay may be about right. If you occasionally need to buy a really expensive item, such as a new car, you can pay the fee to withdraw the money.

For our example, we will assume you keep $4000 in your normal day-to-day account, and put the remainder into redraw. So the salary account will give you offset on around $4000 that you would not otherwise get. This works out to $840 at 7 per cent over the three years. You can ignore the honeymoon rate. This is a gain, so put minus $840 in the standard loan column. The salary account may have extra account keeping fees, but these days most of them don't. Reduce the $840 by the value of these fees over three years if your bank charges them.

For the budget loan, you would be unlikely to be earning interest at a significant rate on this money, as it represents your day-to-day account balance. Most day-to-day bank accounts pay 0.1 per cent if you're lucky. If you do have the money in an account paying interest, then work out the average interest and put this in as a negative amount on the budget loan. Anything you spend you put in as positive, anything you gain as negative.

Now we are ready to add up the three-year cost for each loan.

If you look back at Table 1.5, you will find the budget loan in this case actually costs more than the standard loan, mainly because of the effect of the set-up fee and the salary account. It could be the other way around for you. If you can get a budget loan without the set-up fee, and with a free credit card and free bank account, it would be more attractive. If your mortgage principal is higher than this, it would also make the budget loan more attractive as the interest saving would be higher, whereas the fees and the offset gain would still be the same.

If it seems surprising to you that a budget loan could cost more in some situations, this is because if there was a really marked advantage to one type of loan, everyone would choose it. The higher your mortgage, the more attractive the budget loan becomes because you are saving more in interest. The more perks you can get on your budget loan, the more attractive it becomes. Ask for a budget loan with a zero set-up fee and a free bank account and credit card. You may get it. You can see from the table the difference the salary account makes to the cost of the loan. Don't disregard the value of a salary account when you choose your loan. It can be quite significant.

If you can get an interest rate discount on a standard loan for belonging to a union or professional association, the standard loan is more attractive because this discount does not usually apply on a budget loan. You effectively get the budget loan rate with the standard loan features. If you have this option, then take it. It will win every time.

Applying for a loan

When you have worked out how much you can pay back and which type of loan will suit you best, have your loan pre-approved by your bank before you buy your new home. Most banks will give you this pre-approval in writing. The actual loan approval will still depend on the house you choose, as the bank will need to value the property before they give you the final okay.

With your pre-approval amount in writing, you will know what you can afford, and buyers and estate agents will take you more seriously. A seller (called a vendor in real estate jargon) is usually more willing to accept an offer if the loan amount you need is pre-approved. Your position is almost as good as that of a cash buyer.

Double-check all the fees before you apply for any loan. Ask if you are allowed to make extra payments and if there is a penalty for paying off your loan early.

Many banks have mobile bankers who call on you and arrange the details of your loan. Before you arrange this, though, it is better to get all the information you can, so you know what questions to ask, and can judge if you are getting a good deal.

If you go into a branch and discuss a loan, you are under less commercial pressure than you are with a mobile lender's representative calling on you. You can also apply for a loan over the Internet. It is best to actually talk to someone from the bank before you do this.

If the bank doesn't offer exactly what you want, then ask for it. Banks want your business and are usually prepared to be a bit flexible. Some normal loans offer all sorts of perks that budget loans don't. If you only want one or two of the perks, the bank may be prepared to give them to you with the budget loan.

You can also get your loan through a mortgage broker, and this doesn't usually cost you anything. The mortgage broker has access to a range of lenders and loan types, and knows all the loans and all the rates, perks and fees. He or she will get the best loan for your circumstances. The broker is paid by the institution, not by the customer. You may think that you have to pay for this in the long run, but the institution saves the cost of their own mobile banker coming to you, or their representative talking to you.

Loan approval

Most banks can give you provisional approval within 24 hours and written approval within a few days. The things banks look at when assessing your loan include:

- Your income and your partner's income. You may need to supply a payslip or your employer's details so the bank can check this. If you are self-employed, you will need to show how much you earn in some other way, such as tax returns or a statement from your accountant. Your income may include interest, dividends, family allowance and maintenance payments. If so, include these on your application.
- Your assets: this includes cash, shares, managed investments, superannuation, other residential or commercial property, vehicles, household goods and any other items of value, such as jewellery. If you are owed money (by the tax department, for example), include this here.
- Your family circumstances: such as how many children or other dependents you have, and any maintenance payments you make.
- Your current debt commitments: such as vehicle hire purchase, credit card balances, and personal loans. Include here any tax that you owe or will owe.
- The amount of deposit you have available. At times when it has been available, this can include the government

homebuyer's grant if you qualify for it. You will normally need at least 5 per cent of the purchase price plus enough to cover purchase costs such as stamp duty.

- Where the deposit came from. The bank will look more kindly at your application if you saved the deposit gradually over some time, as this demonstrates your ability to pay your loan. If the deposit is a gift from parents or parents-in-law, or if you can't explain where it currently is or where it is coming from, your application may be viewed less favourably.
- The value of the property you are buying. Usually this will be the purchase price, but the bank may want an independent valuation. Some lenders will not lend money for country properties, or will require a higher deposit.
- Your credit history. A bad credit rating will come back to haunt you for a long time.

The bank may ask you for an estimate of your weekly living expenses. If you keep track of this for a few weeks you should have some idea of the amount. I showed you how to do this when we looked at working out how much you could borrow on page 20. If you can come up with a reasonable figure, it will look better to a bank representative than if you have no idea at all.

If you want to maximise the amount you can borrow, never get a bad credit rating, pay cash for your car, and always pay the full amount on your credit card statement by the date due. The bank will work out the repayment they think you can make, then deduct from this any amount you are paying for your car loan and your credit card repayment if these are applicable. This could considerably reduce the amount you can borrow.

The bank will initially decide how much you can borrow and may give you written approval for that amount. You are not obliged to borrow this amount. You can borrow a lesser amount if you want to. Don't just assume at this point that you will get the loan and make a cash offer for a home. The bank will need to value the particular property before they will give final approval for your loan.

Mortgages on the Internet

All of the major Australian banks have websites with a lot of information on their loan products. There are also specialist mortgage sites and there are even online mortgage brokers who will take your details and find the cheapest loan option for you. If you feel you would like help with your decision, you may like to contact a broker in this way. There are some sites giving a comparison between the rates and features of loans offered by different banks.

You can apply for your loan online if you want to, but most bank Internet sites do not give you the fine detail on their loan products and offset accounts, so it is best to talk to a loan representative at your bank or a mobile banker before you apply.

Most bank sites have calculators so you can estimate how much you can borrow, what the repayments will be, and even the purchase costs. Most state and territory government websites have the information necessary to calculate how much stamp duty you will pay on the house purchase and the mortgage.

Website addresses and website content are constantly changing. The best way to find available sites is by searching. Try 'home loan' or 'mortgage' and 'Australia'. I have included a list of websites that are relevant at time of writing at the back of this book. I have included banks, non-bank lenders and mortgage brokers. This list is not exhaustive. There are many other sources of finance, such as smaller credit unions. Some estate agents and builders have their own finance providers, and can arrange your loan for you.

Transferring your loan

If you move house, you can usually take your loan along with you. This is called portability and, while it sounds good, it is really only a minor perk. The fees vary for this, but are usually less than setting up a new loan. You may also save on mortgage stamp duty.

However, you may want to take the opportunity to look around at what other banks are offering, and you may get a loan with a zero set-up fee and the honeymoon rate if you start again on a new loan.

Refinancing your loan

Keep up to date with available loans even when you are paying your loan off. It may pay to change banks if another bank has a really good deal. If you have access to the Internet, check out some mortgage comparison sites occasionally to make sure that you are still getting a good deal on your loan.

You can change your loan type at your current bank by paying any set-up fees for the new loan and any penalty for early termination of your previous loan type (this will usually only apply to fixed rate loans). You will not have to pay mortgage stamp duty again if you stay with the same bank. Ask your bank to give you all the costs involved, in writing, before you go ahead with the transfer.

You may get a better deal by refinancing with another bank, as they have more to gain by you transferring than your own bank does by you changing loan types.

If you refinance your loan with another bank, you may need to pay the mortgage stamp duty again. This varies between states and territories, so check with your bank. You may also have to pay mortgage insurance again if you are borrowing more than 80 per cent of the value of your home. Your home may have gone up in value since you first bought it, and you may have paid off some of the principal, so this may not turn out to be a problem. Again, get all the costs, in writing, from the new bank.

Work out whether the interest saving over the first three years is greater than the sum of the transfer costs, the mortgage stamp duty, and the mortgage insurance if this applies to you. Work out the interest saving on the current loan balance as this is quite accurate enough. If you are getting the honeymoon rate for the first year with the new bank, it may well be worthwhile changing banks.

Keep in mind that if you currently have a free credit card and a transaction-fee-free account with your bank, you would need to transfer these accounts to the new bank. If you have lots of payments automatically paid into or taken from your account, changing these payments may be rather time consuming. You will need to ensure that every automatic payment is taken care of when you transfer.

Home loan rates don't vary much between banks and other mortgage providers, because there is so much competition between them. Banks want to lend you money. This is how they make their profits. Remember that the bank is not doing you a favour by lending you money. You are doing them a favour by choosing to borrow from them.

Buying a home 2

When buying a home, try to get the best deal you can for both the cost of the house and the cost of the home loan. This will give you a head start in paying off your mortgage.

Put down as much deposit as you can possibly scrape together without leaving yourself short of cash. Most banks and lending institutions will charge mortgage insurance if you borrow more than 80 per cent of the price of the home. This can be quite expensive and is worth saving. It is worth renting for a bit longer while you save the deposit.

If you or your partner have never owned or part-owned a house before, you may be eligible for a government grant ($7000 at the time of writing). This will help to cover the initial costs. The amount and availability of this grant may change with government policy. The money will be paid when the house purchase is settled, so you cannot rely on it to pre-pay stamp duty or for the initial deposit you pay when you sign a contract to buy the house.

If you get your loan pre-approved, you are practically a cash buyer and should be able to do a better deal than just paying the asking price for your new home. Allow extra to cover the cost of settlement and the stamp duty on the house transaction and the mortgage. This can be around $7000 or more on an average home, so don't disregard it. I will show you how to calculate these costs a little further on. You will also need to have the house insured, so allow for this too.

Try to have at least another $1000 available in case repairs are needed when you move into the house. If you were previously renting you may also need to buy new furniture, a washing machine or a lawnmower.

How much can you pay for your home?

Your first step is to work out what you can afford. This is the most important aspect of choosing a home. We would all like to live in a magnificent house in a top suburb, but you are wasting your own and everyone else's time if you look at houses you can't afford to buy.

In the last chapter I showed you how to work out what you could afford to borrow. Add your deposit to this amount to work out the total amount you can spend, remembering to allow for the purchase costs, and the first home buyers' rebate if you are eligible for this.

Purchase costs

The costs of buying a home vary a little between states and territories, as different rates of tax apply. The costs you will incur when buying a house include settlement agent's or solicitor's fees, land transfer fees, a proportion of the council rates and taxes for the portion of the year you own the home, and stamp duty on the transaction. You may want to get a pest or building inspection before you commit to the purchase.

There is no GST on the sale of residential property at the time of writing.

Stamp duty on the house transaction is calculated differently for different states and territories, and is on a sliding scale, so you pay a different percentage for each portion of the total. Your estate agent or settlement agent will give you a table for your state or territory, so you don't need to calculate it. The stamp duty figures for purchasers can also be found on the government website for most states and territories. Most governments have some sort of concession for low-income families buying their first home if the house is below a certain value.

There are also costs to set up your loan. These include loan set-up fees, registration of mortgage and mortgage stamp duty.

The stamp duty on mortgages also varies between states and territories. Your bank or mortgage provider will be able to give you the formula for your state or territory and, again, the rates will be on your government's website. Mortgage stamp duty may be eliminated in 2005 as part of the GST-related tax changes.

When you move in, you will have other costs that need to be paid, such as transfer fees for water, gas, power and telephone, and removalist fees. You will need to pay for your mail to be redirected. You may need to buy bottled gas or firewood if the house is new or the previous owners have let these run out. If you are currently renting, you may need to have the carpets shampooed and the flues cleaned at the rental property. All this can add up to several hundred dollars that you will have to find from somewhere. It may be several weeks before your rental bond is returned to you.

Keep enough aside for all these costs and enough for emergencies. If you find you have set aside too much when you have moved in and paid all the costs, just add the excess to your first mortgage payment.

Typical costs

Table 2.1 shows some typical costs for buying a home worth around $180 000 with a loan of $150 000. Remember that the stamp duty on the purchase and the mortgage vary between states and territories and with the value of the home. The conveyancing fee is the amount paid to the settlement agent or solicitor for transferring the property and dealing with the payment. Find the figures for your state and your price range. Don't just use mine, as they may be different.

Make sure you take these costs into account when you decide how much you can afford to pay for a home.

Table 2.1 Typical purchase costs

Item	**$**
Conveyancing fees	400
Land transfer	100
Rates and taxes	500
Stamp duty on purchase	5000
Loan set-up fee	600
Registration of mortgage	100
Mortgage stamp duty	600
Total costs	**7300**

Choosing your home

Choose your location

Spend some time looking around suburbs before you buy. You normally pay more for a home close to the city, in certain desirable areas such as along seashores and river fronts, and in areas that are being redeveloped from older houses on larger blocks to groups of home units. Most cities, however, have suburbs that are quite pleasant but not as expensive. There may be a street or two of smaller, older houses in an otherwise top suburb, and a suburb just outside the current fashionable fringe could appreciate in value considerably in a few years' time.

Drive and walk through your chosen area at various times of the week. A suburb that is quiet on a Sunday may be bedlam mid-week with an adjacent noisy industry. Check out the local shops and schools, the bus or train services, and the route you would take to and from work.

Look over any homes that are open in the area, even if they are slightly outside your price range. That way you learn to judge what a home in that suburb is worth.

Choose your features

Think carefully about what you want in a home and make a list of features you would like. You may need to make compromises, but some compromises are better than others. If you want a dishwasher, for example, and homes in your price range don't come with dishwashers, a home with a spot where you could install a dishwasher is a better choice than a home where you would need to rebuild the kitchen to fit one in.

Be realistic about what you can afford. You may have to start with less house than you would have liked. Be positive about what you can achieve in terms of doing the house up to suit you, instead of having an 'is-this-all-we-can-afford' attitude. Almost any house with a garden can be made to look neat and attractive, and small kitchens are perfectly adequate if you don't clutter them with unused kitchen gadgets. Professional carpet cleaning can do a surprisingly good job on grubby carpets, and fresh light-coloured paint can make the dingiest house look clean. Skylights installed in dim houses can brighten up the house no end. Enterprising owners of small homes can make excellent use of odd corners and outdoor areas.

If what you want is more space than homes in your price bracket usually run to, then a bit of patience may allow you to find a larger but run-down home in your chosen area. Most people buying established homes redecorate their home in the first couple of years anyway.

Think about whether you could extend the home later if you wanted to. Is there space on the block to do this? It may be cheaper to extend than to move house, particularly if your home is in a quality suburb or in a location that you particularly like.

Look over your chosen home a second time before you make an offer. If you're unsure, take someone with you who is experienced in home ownership. Look for signs of dampness on ceilings, below sinks and on walls on the other side of shower recesses. Cracks and leaks may be fixable, but this is all extra cost when you move in.

Check the general maintenance level of the house. Look for dripping taps, peeling paint, doors that stick, gutters full of leaves. These sorts of things indicate that the owners have not cared for the house and that you may be buying problems. On the other hand, you may get the house for less. Houses that have had a quick paint job and tidy-up before selling do fetch a higher price because buyers find them more attractive. If you are prepared to take on a run-down home, put in a low offer. The vendors may be fed up by then with purchasers turning up their noses at peeling paint and dirty carpets.

Think about resale value when you buy a home. Something trendy may appeal to you now, but it may be dated and hard to sell in ten years' time.

Making an offer

Start by making a low offer for the home. You can always increase your offer, but you can't decrease it. Houses are usually on the market for some weeks and the asking price is normally higher than the vendors expect to get. Although the estate agent is technically working for the vendor, it is in his or her interest to actually make a sale, rather than to get the best price. The commission is paid when the house is sold, and it does not vary much for small differences in the price of the home.

Don't criticise the house in front of the owners, or they may resent selling it to you. If you say you are over the moon about buying their house but unfortunately can't quite afford their price, you are more likely to get your offer accepted.

People selling homes are often in a hurry for one reason or another. They may have changed their employment to another area, or signed to buy another house. Some perfectly nice houses can take a long time to sell and vendors may become discouraged, fed up with the whole deal, and willing to sell at a lower price to someone enthusiastic about their home. You can afford to be patient when you make an offer. Unless the house is under-priced to start with, there will rarely be a queue of willing buyers. Under-priced houses are rare these days; estate agents know what houses are worth. Most houses are sold through agents and houses sold privately by the owners are more often over-priced than under-priced.

When you make an offer, the vendor will usually come

back with a counter-offer somewhere in between the original price and your offer. Try another offer a bit lower than this. The agent wants a sale and will try to persuade both parties to agree to a price.

If you are buying at an auction, stick to the price you want to pay. There are always other homes available. For ordinary families buying ordinary homes, the choice is normally fairly good. If you must have this particular home for one reason or another, you may well end up paying more at an auction than the home is worth.

What happens next

When your offer has been accepted, you will need to contact your bank and make a formal application for the loan. Provided the bank values the home at approximately what you are offering, and your circumstances have not changed since you first applied for a loan, the approval should take no more than a week or so.

The actual contract of sale varies a little between states and territories. It will also depend whether you are buying your house at an auction. If you are not familiar with the buying and selling process, your estate agent will explain it to you. All contracts follow the same basic pattern. You make an offer for a home, subject to finance and any other conditions, such as pest or building inspections, and the vendor accepts it. At some point in the process, when all conditions are met and the contract has been signed by both parties, the transaction becomes unconditional and legally binding.

A solicitor or settlement agent will arrange the conveyancing of the property. Conveyancing is the actual transfer of the title to your name and the payment to the vendor of your deposit and the loan amount from your bank. The solicitor or settlement agent will calculate the proportion of council rates that you owe, arrange any papers you need to sign for the land transfer, pay the required stamp duty and pay the estate agent their commission. You will be given a statement showing details of all the payments. The title to your property will be retained by the bank until you have paid off the loan.

You will normally collect the key for your property from the estate agent on the day the transaction is settled and the money changes hands. The home is now yours, and so is the mortgage.

If you are buying at an auction you normally need to pay 10 per cent deposit if your bid is accepted. Make sure you have this amount readily available. Talk to the estate agent who is organising the auction beforehand. He or she will be able to give you details of the auction procedure.

Things can sometimes go wrong

Most transactions go through perfectly smoothly, but occasionally there can be minor hitches and, once in a while, major hitches.

The vendor may have several offers and is not obliged to accept yours even if it is for the full asking price. They may have a cash offer, or even an offer for a price higher than the asking price. After the vendor has accepted your offer it is still possible for them to sell the property to someone else in some circumstances, if the contract has not been finalised or all conditions have not yet been met. This is called 'gazumping'. Your estate agent can give you information about this, as the laws for real estate contracts vary between states and territories.

Fixtures are normally sold with the home. This usually

includes everything fixed to the house in some way. There are some borderline things, however. You would not expect a washing machine to come with the home, for example, yet a dishwasher normally will, and there is really no difference in the fixings. Make sure any fittings that are to be left in the home are listed on the contract, as disputes are common. There can be no dispute if the item is listed in writing.

It can be quite stressful waiting for your loan approval and your purchase to be settled. It is stressful for the vendor, too. There are cases where people sign for homes when they don't actually have enough money to buy them, so the transaction is cancelled at the last minute. The vendor may have a legal claim to compensation in such a case. White ants could turn up in the pest inspection, and most vendors are also purchasing another home to move into, so they have purchasing worries too.

If you are currently renting, allow a day or two extra when you give your notice in case settlement is delayed and you cannot move in on the day you expect to. A few days' rent is a small price to pay to be free from worry over moving dates, and gives you extra time to move your things and clean both the house you are moving to and the house you were renting.

If things do go wrong (and usually they don't), just accept it and start again on your house hunting. Don't get discouraged. Buying and selling property is stressful for everyone. Another wonderful home is out there waiting for you to come along and buy it.

3 Fast-track your mortgage

There are three ways you can save money on your mortgage:

1. Start by getting the cheapest mortgage you possibly can. Keep track of mortgage options and be prepared to change if you will save money.
2. Control your day-to-day cash efficiently so that you keep as much money as possible in offset accounts.
3. Reduce the amount you spend so you have more money to put into offset accounts or use for extra mortgage payments.

In Chapter 1 we looked at choosing the best mortgage to suit you. In Chapters 4 and 5 I will show you ways to manage money efficiently and to spend less without affecting your enjoyment of life. In this chapter I will show you just how effective offset accounts and extra payments can be in saving you interest.

Why fast-track?

Even small increases in the amount you pay off your mortgage each month can make a huge difference to the total amount you pay. For our example mortgage of $100 000 at 7 per cent over 25 years, paying an extra $192 a month will save you $50 000 in interest payments and you will pay off the loan ten years earlier. That amount is between one and two years' take-home pay for most people; $50 000 would buy you two new cars, fund an extension to your home, or allow you to retire two years earlier—for less than $45 a week extra towards your mortgage payment. And this extra payment does not all have to be cash. Some of it can be gained by having money in an offset account.

Remember our example family back in the introduction who put an extra $300 a month into their mortgage payment, continued to invest the same amount when their mortgage was paid off, and retired with over $1 million dollars.

Extra payments may look impossible to you when you start out, particularly if this is your first home. It is cheaper to rent a house than it is to own one. You will have costs as a home owner that you never had while you were renting; such as council rates and house insurance, and the extra costs of buying the home (stamp duty and so forth) may have been more than you expected. The affordable suburbs for first homebuyers get further and further from city centres, so you may have extra transport costs to work.

All this may make any extra payment at all look about as easy as a trip to the moon. The important thing is to put in what you can and to keep motivated. The extra will get easier and easier as time goes on. Any extra at all is a big gain. Don't be discouraged by the huge size of your debt compared to your payment. Think in terms of the amount you have managed to pay off and the interest you will save, not the amount you still owe. Every extra dollar you can put into your mortgage brings you closer to the time when your mortgage is paid off and your money can be saved and invested to fund your retirement. Every single extra dollar helps.

Saving time and money with extra payments

Table 3.1 shows the amount of interest and pay-off time you will save with various extra amounts added to your payment each month for our example $100 000 loan at 7 per cent. This extra does not necessarily have to be extra cash. You may be able to arrange your banking so part of your extra is in offset (see p 10), rather than cash payment. An average balance of around $1700 in a salary account on a 7 per cent mortgage is equivalent to paying an extra $10 per month off your loan.

The first column of Table 3.1 is the extra payment per month, the second the number of years it will take to pay off the loan, the third the number of years you will save and the last column is the total interest saving. So that you can compare the saving to the original interest amount, the total interest payable if the loan is paid off over 25 years is around $112 000. An extra $250 a month will save you over half of this.

I have included this table using a range of interest rates in the Tables section near the back of this book. Select the table for the interest rate closest to yours, work out how much extra you can put in on average and you can look up the time and dollar amount you will save.

If you pay your mortgage fortnightly or weekly, multiply your extra payment by 2.17 for fortnightly and 4.33 for weekly. If your principal differs from $100 000, you can work out the extra you need to find for the same effect by simple scaling. If your loan is for $150 000, then multiply the extra payment in the table by 1.5, and the interest you save by 1.5. The payout time stays the same.

Table 3.1 Time and interest saving for extra mortgage payments

Extra per mth $	Yrs to payout	Yrs saved	Amt saved $
10	24.1	0.9	4 868
20	23.2	1.8	9 276
50	21.1	3.9	20 353
100	18.4	6.6	33 949
150	16.4	8.6	43 801
200	14.8	10.2	51 321
250	13.5	11.5	57 275
300	12.4	12.6	62 120
400	10.7	14.3	69 552
500	9.5	15.5	75 004
600	8.5	16.5	79 186
700	7.7	17.3	82 501
800	7.0	18.0	85 195
900	6.5	18.5	87 429
1000	6.0	19.0	89 314

So for a $150 000 mortgage, an extra $450 per month will reduce the term as for an extra $300 in the table and save you $93 180 in interest ($62 120 × 1.5).

You will also be saving ongoing loan fees for the years you are no longer paying off the loan. This could save around another $100 per year.

The diminishing returns effect

You may notice from the table that there is a diminishing returns effect with extra mortgage payments. An extra $250 a month saves you over $57 000 in interest, whereas a further $250 a month (so you are paying $500 extra) only saves a

Spreadsheet tip

To set up this table on an Excel spreadsheet you need to calculate the number of payments you would make to pay off a given loan amount with a set payment. The formula for calculating the number of payments is not as straightforward as the formula to calculate the payment amount:

$$n = \frac{\ln (a / (a - P \times r))}{\ln (1 + r)}$$

n is the number of payments
a is the payment amount
P is the principal
r is the interest rate per period
ln is the natural log function

The spreadsheet function for this formula is called NPER. For Excel the syntax for NPER is:

= NPER(interest rate, payment amount, present value, future value, type)

Use the interest rate per month. The present value is the amount of your loan and the future value is zero because you will have paid the loan off at the end of the term. The type is zero as we are making the payment at the end of the month.

When you know the number of repayments for your new repayment amount, you can work out how long it will take you to pay off the loan.

You can also work out the total that you would pay by multiplying the payment amount by the number of payments. Subtract this total from the amount you would have paid if you had paid the normal repayment. This would be the standard repayment multiplied by 300 months. This gives you the interest saving.

This is a more complex spreadsheet, so don't attempt it unless you are experienced in Excel.

further $18 000. Does this mean there is a point where it is better to do something else with the money than paying off the mortgage? The answer is no.

While this diminishing returns effect may seem rather surprising, there are two reasons for it. The first is that the interest component of your payment is higher in the early years of your loan, forming a higher proportion of the total interest you pay. Whether you pay $250 extra or $500 extra in the first year, the extra you are paying is still only a small proportion of the total principal at this stage, so the interest saving is also only a small proportion. Once you have paid the interest for a given year, you can never go back and reduce this amount.

The second reason is that if you pay $500 extra per month, you will pay off your mortgage sooner, so you will have fewer payments than you would with $250 extra. You are paying the higher amount for less time, so you are not paying twice as much extra payment overall. Remember each payment is your base payment plus the extra, so each payment you save is worth much more than just the extra amount.

The saving in interest is also only the first part of the story. When you have paid off your loan, you are going to invest the money that you were using for the loan payment. The faster you pay off the loan, the sooner you will have money to invest, and the more interest you will earn.

What this effect does mean is that even a small extra contribution goes a long way in saving you money, and the earlier you put in the extra, the more you save.

Invest in your mortgage

Paying off your mortgage is usually the best way to invest any extra money you are able to save. There are some exceptions to this, which we will cover later in this chapter but, in general, the advantages of extra payments favour mortgages—not just on a return for money basis, but also for ease of investment, convenience, family allowance and tax benefit purposes and liquidity. Liquidity is the ease with which you can convert your investments to cash.

The first thing we need to understand is why paying off a mortgage can be considered as a return on money invested, when you are actually paying money out, not gaining interest income. You need to think of a return on money as the net amount of extra money that you gain when you invest the money or use it to pay off a loan.

Suppose you have $1000 in a bank term deposit paying 5 per cent interest. At the end of the year, your $50 interest is paid by the bank, and you are $50 better off (less tax).

Now suppose you use that $1000 as a payment on a mortgage at 7 per cent interest. That's $1000 that you are no longer paying interest on, so you pay $70 less interest, leaving you $70 better off at the end of the year. You owe $70 less than if you had not made the payment. There is no tax to pay on this $70, because it is not considered as income. The return to you on that $1000 is 7 per cent, and the return is just as real as the return on the term deposit.

Advantages

The advantages of paying off your mortgage with any extra money you can save are:

- The after tax return on your savings is equivalent to the mortgage rate. Very few other safe investments can offer this.
- Making extra payments is easy and convenient. You can add what you like when you like.

- The return is predictable. It will vary with mortgage rates, but has no other market fluctuations.
- The return is low risk. Your money can never be lost. Even if your house burnt down or was lost in a landslide, provided it was insured, you would get more of the insurance payout and the bank would get less.
- You can put small amounts of money into your loan. Most other investment types need a large initial investment amount. You can vary the extra amount you put into your loan to suit you.
- The return on your savings is not only tax free, it doesn't increase your income for social security or family tax benefit purposes the way investment income does. Nor is it deemed to be an asset for tax or welfare purposes. It cannot put you into a higher tax bracket, the superannuation surcharge range or the Medicare levy surcharge range or increase your HECS repayment.
- Most loans offer a redraw facility. This means your extra payments are put into a separate account, and you can take the money back out if you need to, usually on short notice. There may be a fee for withdrawal, but most other investments also have withdrawal fees or brokerage charges.
- A redraw account or salary account effectively gives you a bank account with a return equal to the mortgage rate, with no tax to pay on the income.

Look back at Table 3.1 showing the amount of interest you would save by paying extra each month. That saving may not be money in your pocket right now, but it is still money you will have at some time in your life that you would not have had if you had not chosen to fast-track.

Keep in mind that everything you manage to save on your home loan interest is tax-free extra money for you. Also remember that in 25 years' time, the value of your home will be exactly the same whether you paid $50 000 interest on your loan by paying it off over twelve years with an extra $300 per month, or $112 000 interest paying it off over 25 years. The extra $62 000 interest does not increase the value of your home by even one dollar.

How to fast-track

To fast-track your mortgage you can make extra payments, or you can keep money in an offset account, where the balance on your account is taken from the amount you owe before the interest is calculated on your mortgage. Offset accounts (discussed in detail on p 10) are really the same as paying more off your mortgage. You are effectively earning interest on the money at the home loan rate and paying this interest amount off your loan. There are some variations on both these methods.

The extra payments you make can be a regular amount that you add to your payment each month, or occasional payments when you have unexpected or extra income. In Chapter 5 I will give you some ideas on where to find the extra. This section will show you how and why it works.

Try to add at least 10 per cent of your take-home pay to your mortgage payment if you can possibly manage this. If your family has a second income, then also add at least 25 per cent of the second amount.

For example, if you have a take-home pay of $3000 per month, then try to add $300 per month to the payment. If you are paid fortnightly, then multiply 10 per cent of your fortnightly pay by 2.17 to give the extra monthly amount. Multiply by 4.33 if you are paid weekly. Throughout this section I have assumed an extra payment of $300 per month on our $100 000 mortgage. Even if your amounts differ from the examples, the method works just the same. You can use the tables or the spreadsheet calculations at the end of this book to work out the values for your own mortgage and your own extra payments. You can even set up your own personal loan table to keep track of how you are going on a payment by payment basis.

The real cost of a home loan

When you have a normal principal and interest home loan over a period of 25 years, most of what you pay in the first few years is interest. This is because the payments are constant throughout the loan, but the interest on the remaining amount that you owe decreases as the balance owing decreases.

For example, if you have a loan of $100 000 at 7 per cent, in the first year the interest is going to be around $7000. The total of payments for the year is around $8500, so you have paid the interest, and around $1500 off your principal. By the end of year 20, you may have paid off around $65 000, so the interest on the amount you still owe will be 7 per cent of $35 000, which is around $2500, leaving $6000 of your $8500 to pay off the principal.

You will find that after five years you have paid only a few thousand dollars off your loan, although you have paid tens of thousands in payments.

Table 3.2 shows each year of our example home loan, paid at the normal rate. The payment per month for this loan is around $707. You may also pay a loan fee of $5 to $10 a month. I have ignored these loan fees in the calculations.

The Owing column is the amount you owe at the beginning of the year. The next two columns are the amount of principal you pay off during the year and the amount of interest. The Total paid and the Total interest columns are the total amount you have paid since the start date. The last column gives the principal owing at the end of the year.

By the end of the fifth year, you will have paid $42 407 in payments, but you will have paid only $8838 off your loan.

At the end of the 25 years, you will have repaid your original $100 000 plus over $112 000 in interest, more than the amount you borrowed. If interest rates go up to 10 per cent, this interest figure goes up to $172 600, and for 12 per cent, it reaches $216 000.

If you look at Table 3.2 carefully, you will find that it is over 15 years before even half of your loan payment is going towards repaying the principal. You can also see that it is over 17 years before you have paid off half of the original amount.

If you pay the same loan off over 30 years, your repayment amount will be reduced to $665, but the total interest you pay will be over $139 000.

If you want to set up your own worksheet, either on a home computer or using a calculator with the values for your own loan, I have included a section on spreadsheets at the end of the book with detailed instructions. Or you can download this spreadsheet from my webpage and put in your own values for principal and interest rate. See the Useful Websites section for the address for the downloads.

I have also included tables at the back of this book for a loan of $100 000 for a range of interest rates. There is also

Table 3.2 Loan of $100 000 at 7%, paid off over 25 years

Year	Owing	Principal	Interest	Total paid	Total int	Now owe
1	100 000	1530	6952	8 481	6 952	98 470
2	98 470	1640	6841	16 963	13 792	96 830
3	96 830	1759	6722	25 444	20 515	95 071
4	95 071	1886	6595	33 925	27 110	93 185
5	93 185	2022	6459	42 407	33 569	91 162
6	91 162	2169	6313	50 888	39 882	88 993
7	88 993	2325	6156	59 369	46 037	86 668
8	86 668	2494	5988	67 851	52 025	84 174
9	84 174	2674	5808	76 332	57 833	81 501
10	81 501	2867	5614	84 814	63 447	78 633
11	78 633	3074	5407	93 295	68 854	75 559
12	75 559	3297	5185	101 776	74 039	72 262
13	72 262	3535	4946	110 258	78 985	68 727
14	68 727	3791	4691	118 739	83 676	64 937
15	64 937	4065	4417	127 220	88 093	60 872
16	60 872	4358	4123	135 702	92 216	56 514
17	56 514	4673	3808	144 183	96 023	51 841
18	51 841	5011	3470	152 664	99 494	46 829
19	46 829	5374	3108	161 146	102 601	41 456
20	41 456	5762	2719	169 627	105 321	35 694
21	35 694	6179	2303	178 108	107 624	29 515
22	29 515	6625	1856	186 590	109 480	22 890
23	22 890	7104	1377	195 071	110 857	15 786
24	15 786	7618	864	203 552	111 721	8168
25	8 168	8168	313	212 034	112 034	0

a table showing the time and interest saving for a range of extra payments for each interest rate.

To calculate the total interest you will pay for your own loan, just multiply the standard amount you pay each month by the number of months (usually 300) and take away the amount you originally borrowed. This will give you the total interest you would pay if you paid the loan off normally. This assumes, of course, that the rate always stays the same. If you are on a lower honeymoon rate for the first year, multiply the first year's monthly payment by 12, and then multiply the second year's payment by the remaining months (usually 288) to get the total amount.

For an interest only loan, you pay only the interest so the principal remains the same. The interest remains constant as long as the rate doesn't change. You never pay off this type of loan unless you choose to pay it off in full, or convert it to a normal loan at some point.

Paying your loan off early

The value of paying your home loan off early is in the interest that you will save. This money could be invested and working hard to fund your retirement, instead of being paid to the bank.

If you paid the loan in Table 3.2 off in 13 years, by increasing your payment by $300 to $1007 per month, you would save around $62 000 in interest. If you then put the $1007 per month into an investment at 6 per cent for the remaining twelve years of the original loan term, you would have over $212 000.

If you kept saving at this rate, in another five years you would have over $355 000 and after ten years you would have nearly $550 000. After 15 years you would have $812 000. If you started at age 25 and retired at 65, this would be your retirement amount. If your return on savings was 7 per cent rather than 6 per cent, the amount is $964 000, and for 8 per cent it is $1 157 000.

Table 3.3 Loan of $100 000 at 7%, with $300 extra payment

Yr	Owing	Princ	Interest	Tot paid	Tot int	Now owe
1	100 000	5 248	6834	12 081	6 834	94 752
2	94 752	5 627	6454	24 163	13 288	89 125
3	89 125	6 034	6048	36 244	19 336	83 092
4	83 092	6 470	5611	48 325	24 947	76 622
5	76 622	6 938	5144	60 407	30 091	69 684
6	69 684	7 439	4642	72 488	34 733	62 245
7	62 245	7 977	4104	84 569	38 838	54 268
8	54 268	8 554	3528	96 651	42 366	45 715
9	45 715	9 172	2909	108 732	45 275	36 543
10	36 543	9 835	2246	120 814	47 521	26 708
11	26 708	10 546	1535	132 895	49 057	16 162
12	16 162	11 308	773	144 976	49 830	4 854
13	4 854	4 854	84	149 915	49 914	0

Table 3.3 shows the same loan paid off more quickly by adding $300 to the monthly payment.

This table shows it is less than four years before half your payment is going towards repaying the principal, and you will have paid off half the amount in less than eight years. If you pay a monthly fee for your loan, you will be saving another $1000 or more in fees by paying the loan off early.

Thirteen years is still a long time, but we can improve on this by using offset accounts. If you average $10 000 in an offset account as well as making the extra payments, you reduce the loan by a further year and your interest total by another $4600.

If $10 000 offset as well as the extra payments seems impossible to you now, remember that this is an average over the life of the loan. If you were saving for a car over a few years, you could easily have this much in offset.

If you are using a redraw account or a salary account rather than actually paying the extra off your loan, the difference between offset and repayment becomes blurred. The extra $10 000 in offset is the same as paying around $60 more per month on your loan. Just keep putting as much extra money as you can into the redraw account, and the extra mortgage payments will look after themselves.

These figures are for a $100 000 loan. If your loan is higher than this, you will need to scale the amounts to have a similar time saving. For a $200 000 loan, for example, you would need to make extra payments of $600 per month for the same effect.

This is your aim. If you can do better than this, great! If you can't do as well, you will still be better off than putting in no extra at all. You may find the extra becomes easier and easier over the years, if your rate of pay increases.

The value of offset

If you have an offset account, then you gain extra without it forming part of your monthly cash payment. The value of the offset can be calculated quite simply as the average amount in your account multiplied by the offset rate. For a mortgage at 7 per cent, to have the equivalent of an extra $10 a month towards your payment, you need an average of $1714 in an account with full offset for the month. You can work out the value of your offset amount each month by multiplying your average balance (estimate this) by your offset rate, then dividing by 12 for one month's value. For example, for an average balance of $1000 and a rate of 7 per cent, your offset is $70 for the year, or around $6 for the month.

Table 3.4 Offset balance required for $10 extra per month loan payment

Rate %	Amount $	Rate %	Amount $
5.00	2400	7.75	1548
5.25	2286	8.00	1500
5.50	2182	8.25	1455
5.75	2087	8.50	1412
6.00	2000	8.75	1371
6.25	1920	9.00	1333
6.50	1846	9.25	1297
6.75	1778	9.50	1263
7.00	1714	9.75	1231
7.25	1655	10.00	1200
7.50	1600		

Table 3.5 Value per month of $1000 offset balance

Rate %	Amount $	Rate %	Amount $
5.00	4.17	7.75	6.46
5.25	4.38	8.00	6.67
5.50	4.58	8.25	6.88
5.75	4.79	8.50	7.08
6.00	5.00	8.75	7.29
6.25	5.21	9.00	7.50
6.50	5.42	9.25	7.71
6.75	5.63	9.50	7.92
7.00	5.83	9.75	8.13
7.25	6.04	10.00	8.33
7.50	6.25		

Tables 3.4 and 3.5 will help you work out the per payment value of your offset account balance for an account with full offset. Table 3.4 gives the amount you need in your offset account to equal a $10 extra payment on your mortgage for a range of interest rates. Table 3.5 gives the extra payment equivalent of each $1000 in your account.

Payoff times

Don't go totally overboard trying to pay extra off your home loan to save all these thousands of dollars. You will not pay your loan off by next week or next year. Life is about living well now, as well as planning to live well in the future. But try to take advantage of every option you have to reduce the loan, especially offset accounts that cost you nothing but can save you a lot. Unless your loan is already substantially paid off, or the remaining balance is very low because you bought your home a long time ago, ten to fifteen years is a reasonable aim.

If you wanted to pay your loan off in one year, you would need to pay back the whole $100 000 as well as the interest in one year. If you wanted to pay it off in two years, you would need to pay $50 000 in principal each year as well as the interest. For three years it would be $33 000. Not many families have this amount over each year, although you might manage it if you put all of a second income into your mortgage. For an average family with one income and two or three small children, paying off the average mortgage (around $150 000) in less than five years is totally unrealistic. Aim for ten years as a best shot, and consider yourself as doing really well if you manage less than this.

Table 3.6 Repayment amounts for a set number of years

AMOUNT = 100 000
RATE = 7%

Years	Per month	Years	Per month	Years	Per month
1	8653	11	1088	21	758
2	4477	12	1028	22	743
3	3088	13	978	23	730
4	2395	14	935	24	718
5	1980	15	899	25	707
6	1705	16	867	26	697
7	1509	17	840	27	688
8	1363	18	816	28	680
9	1251	19	794	29	672
10	1161	20	775	30	665

You may prefer to aim for a certain number of years and set your payment to suit. Table 3.6 shows the repayment amounts for paying the $100 000 loan off over various numbers of years. I have included this table for a range of interest rates at the back of this book.

If your loan is for a different amount, just scale the payment. For a $150 000 loan, multiply the repayment amount by 1.5, for example.

You can see from Table 3.6 that it is more difficult to come down by one year the further down you go. To reduce your mortgage from 30 to 29 years costs only $7 per month more. To reduce from three to two years takes nearly $1400 per month more.

This table just uses the repayment calculation that we covered earlier, except that this time you vary the number of payments. Remember we work in months, so multiply the years by 12 for the number of payments.

Be realistic

To keep pay-off times in perspective, here are some things to think about. The average annual wage in Australia is somewhere in the region of $40 000. Not everyone earns this much, and a lot of families have only one income or one income and a little bit. Many two-income families have considerable childcare costs that reduce the value of the second income. Two-income families are also more likely to rely on fast food and to pay for services such as housework, gardening and window-cleaning.

The home loan amount for the average family is around $150 000. That is over three times the gross annual pay for the average earner. However much extra you put into your mortgage, you are not going the pay it off by next year. You can save a considerable amount of interest by making extra payments, but you can never reduce the total principal that you pay back. If you won Lotto and paid back your loan the week after you bought your house, you would still pay back all of the original principal.

The fact that you can take out a mortgage for more than you can pay back in a short time allows you to live in your home now, rather than waiting for years and years while you save the money to buy it directly. Don't lose sight of this.

I am not trying to dampen your enthusiasm for fast-tracking your mortgage but am stressing the point that you need to keep your payout times in perspective. Don't lose enthusiasm because the amount you pay back in the first few years is depressingly small in comparison to what you owe, in spite of the marathon efforts you are making to put every cent you can into your mortgage. Have patience. You will get there!

Hints and tips

The biggest hurdle is motivation. If you decide just to add what is left over of your pay to your mortgage payment each month, you will get nowhere. There may be nothing over. Decide the amount you are adding and pay it in, preferably on the day you get paid, then manage on what's left.

If you can't add as much as I suggest, or as much as you would like, then add what you can. Any extra is saving you more down the track. Don't be discouraged if the $300 a month extra that I have suggested is way beyond your means. Just do your best. Paying off your mortgage early is a personal achievement, or better still a family achievement, not a race or an attempt for the world record.

Work out some incentive schemes. If you manage the planned extra every month for a year, then have a special family dinner, or a visit to the beach.

You may have the option of paying your mortgage weekly or fortnightly, instead of monthly. This is great if you are paid weekly or fortnightly. A trick that is popular is to divide the monthly amount by two for fortnightly or by four for weekly and pay this amount each time. This means you pay $\frac{1}{24}$ of the total yearly amount each fortnight, so over 26 fortnights you pay two extra fortnightly payments. This alone can reduce your payments by over four years and your interest payments by over $23 000 for the example $100 000 loan.

If you have an offset account, pay for everything you can with a credit card. This gives you extra days with your money in the offset account. This is particularly effective with a salary account, but works for a redraw account too, especially if you are postponing large payments such as council rates or new major appliance costs. Remember you have to pay the credit card balance by the due date so you pay no interest for this to work.

Keeping track

One of the best ways to keep up your motivation is to keep track of how you are going relative to the original term of your loan. Have your bank send you statements as frequently as you can persuade them to. You will have a record of the payments you made and any interest you save with your offset account. If you bank on the Internet, you may be able to have your loan account linked and you can check it as often as you like. You will know from your statement how much you still owe.

If you like rewards, then set up a chart on your pin-up board and tick off every $1000 as your balance owing goes down. You may want to put a coloured star on the chart and write a date next to it. Every $5000, celebrate in some way.

The statement may be all you need to track your mortgage, but you may also want to see where you are in relation to your original loan. For this you will need a spreadsheet for your original amount. You can set up this spreadsheet yourself using the instructions at the end of this book (see p 219), download the spreadsheet from my webpage (see the Useful Websites section) or you can photocopy the worksheet in the Tables section for the interest rate closest to yours.

If you use the tables, go to the last column, the principal now owing, and scale this up or down for the amount of your own loan. If your loan is for $80 000 for example, you multiply the amount in this column by 0.8. If your loan is for $150 000, multiply the amount by 1.5. Write these new amounts in a new column next to the last column. This is your base. When you receive your annual statement, write the amount you still owe in another new column for the current year of your loan and compare it to the base amount. You can work out how much further ahead you are.

You may want to pin up your original loan worksheet and put a star on it and have a party every time your balance reduces to an end of year value. Write the achievement date on as well.

This spreadsheet comparison method does not give you your new payout time. You do, however, know the extra payments you have made towards your loan. Divide the extra amount for the year by 12 to give your average extra monthly payment, then use this in conjunction with the extra payment tables to give you some idea of how much you will save in time and interest. Remember to scale this as the tables are for a $100 000 loan.

If your loan is for $150 000 and your extra is $150 dollars a month, then the equivalent for a loan of $100 000 is $100 extra per month. This will give you the correct time reduction but, for the interest saving, you will have to scale the interest saving amount back up.

The extra that you put in may not be constant, especially if some of it is in offset. Just average the amounts from your statements and you will have a reasonable approximation.

The amount you owe may seem depressingly large for some time. Keep in mind that the average home loan in Australia of around $150 000 is a large amount of money when you think in terms of paying it back. As we saw before, for most people it is three to four years' take-home pay. You don't ever have to face paying this amount back in one hit, so don't think of it like this. It normally takes people most of their working lives to pay off their mortgage. If you can reduce your mortgage payback time by half, this is a huge saving both in time and money. Paying off your mortgage is not something you can do over a short term, but this does not make it a worthless aim, it just makes it a medium- to long-term aim.

What to do if interest rates change

If interest rates go down, continue to put the usual payment into your loan each month. You will be paying the loan off much more quickly by doing this. A 1 per cent drop in interest rates on a $100 000 loan is an extra $1000 a year you will be paying off your loan. Everything you pay off your loan early, especially in the first few years, can save you up to twice that amount over the life of the loan, even more if interest rates are high.

If interest rates go up, try to increase your payment by the extra, rather than relying on the extra payments you make towards your mortgage to cover it.

Your bank will let you know the new minimum payment. The payment at 7 per cent for our standard loan is $707. At 8 per cent the payment is $772, an increase of $65. Increase your payment by the difference.

If interest rates had previously gone down and you left your payment constant, you will only need to increase your payment if the rate goes back above the original level.

When you are nearly there

When the value of the balance in the offset account is equal to the amount that you owe, you will need to actually pay the amount off the mortgage, or take some of the money out of the offset account. If the offset balance exceeds the amount owing, you do not get any benefit on the extra amount, so it may as well be earning interest elsewhere.

For a redraw facility, the mortgage would be paid off automatically at this stage. This will only be a problem if some of the money in the redraw account is actually earmarked for something else. You will need to transfer some of it to another account while you continue to pay off the loan.

When you finally pay out the loan, there may also be a few hundred dollars in discharge fees. Your bank can tell you what these fees will be. The bank will return the title deed to your home and send you a letter of congratulations. The title deed is an important legal document. Store it safely, preferably in a bank safe deposit.

Now have a celebration. There is nothing quite like the freedom feeling of being totally debt-free when you finally fully own your own home. You can now start on phase two of the retirement plan. The real fun begins here.

When you have paid your loan off, invest the money you were paying on your mortgage for your retirement. You have managed without it for this long; you won't miss it now. This amount should allow you to retire reasonably wealthy. Later in Chapter 6 I will give you some ideas for investing your money for your retirement.

You may want to move to a larger home and start mortgage payments again. You will be better at finding the extra by now, and you may have a second income, so the second mortgage should be paid off even more quickly.

Other options

There are four situations where it is better not to fast-track your mortgage with any extra money you have available:

1. if you have other loans at a higher interest rate, for example if you are paying off a credit card balance or have a car on hire purchase;
2. if you can get a better after-tax return than the mortgage rate in other safe investments;
3. if you are borrowing the money to invest in shares or managed funds; or
4. if the loan is for an investment property.

Other loans

If you are paying off a credit card, you are paying around 15 per cent per annum on the outstanding balance in every month in which you don't pay the full amount by the due date. For some department store cards this may be around 20 per cent. For some buy-now-pay-later schemes it can be as high as 25 per cent.

If you are paying for your car on hire purchase, you may be paying from 10 per cent to 12 per cent interest on the loan. You will also be paying a higher insurance premium.

If you are in this situation, pay off the credit card balance or the hire purchase first, then put your savings into your mortgage.

For a credit card, just add any extra you can manage to the payment you make. Get rid of the debt as fast as you can, then start paying your whole card balance when you receive the statement. Every time.

For hire purchase, you may not be able to pay extra unless you can pay out the total outstanding amount. Put your savings into a redraw account on your mortgage then, when you have the required amount, pay out the loan.

If you have a lot of equity in your home (what you owe is less than 60 per cent or so of the value of your house), the bank may be able to combine your loans with your mortgage so you are paying the mortgage rate on all of the outstanding balances. If you choose to do this, make an extra effort to increase the payments, and never run up another credit card balance that you can't pay off when the statement comes.

If you have a loan to run your own business, the interest rate may be higher than for your mortgage. However, the interest will be a tax deduction against your profits, so it will be cheaper finance than the home loan. In this case paying off the mortgage before the business loan is the better option.

Other investments

There are some investments that will give you a higher after-tax return than the mortgage rate, so you may want to look at your other options before you decide to make extra payments on your mortgage. The value of the original amount you owe gets less and less in real terms as the years go by because of inflation, and this may also make it less cost effective to pay off your mortgage.

If the income from an investment puts you into a higher tax bracket, or into the superannuation surcharge range, you may still be better off putting your savings into the mortgage. If one partner has a low income and pays little or no tax, then other investments may be more attractive, but keep in mind any reduction the investment income will make to social security payments or family tax benefits.

The return on paying off your mortgage is reasonably predictable. The return on other types of investment is not always the same from year to year. This makes it more difficult to compare investments with mortgage payout.

Calculating after-tax returns

To be better off investing your money than paying off your mortgage, your after-tax return needs to be higher than the home loan rate. If you are on the normal tax rate (31.5 per cent), your before-tax return would need to be over 10.2 per cent to give you a return equal to a home loan rate of 7 per cent. If you are on the top tax rate, your before-tax return would need to be 13.6 per cent.

To work this return out for your home loan rate, multiply your home loan rate by 100 and divide by the percentage of your pay that you take home (calculated as 100 less your marginal tax rate).

For a 7 per cent loan and a tax rate of 31.5 per cent, the calculation is:

$$\frac{7 \times 100}{68.5} = 10.219$$

Table 3.7 shows the before-tax returns you would need to equal the mortgage rate for various marginal tax rates. Even if your partner's marginal tax rate is zero, he or she may lose spouse rebate, parenting allowance or other welfare benefits for small amounts of income, so don't disregard this.

Table 3.7 Before-tax returns needed on investments to equal mortgage rate

Mortgage rate	Tax rate cents per dollar			
%	18.5	31.5	43.5	48.5
4.0	4.9	5.8	7.1	7.8
4.5	5.5	6.6	8.0	8.7
5.0	6.1	7.3	8.8	9.7
5.5	6.7	8.0	9.7	10.7
6.0	7.4	8.8	10.6	11.7
6.5	8.0	9.5	11.5	12.6
7.0	8.6	10.2	12.4	13.6
7.5	9.2	10.9	13.3	14.6
8.0	9.8	11.7	14.2	15.5
8.5	10.4	12.4	15.0	16.5
9.0	11.0	13.1	15.9	17.5
9.5	11.7	13.9	16.8	18.4
10.0	12.3	14.6	17.7	19.4

If you feel that you can get this return on a safe and stable investment, then invest your spare money rather then paying it off your mortgage. However, read the section on Borrowing to Invest on page 86, as you may be better off restructuring your loan by paying it off, then borrowing against the equity in your home for the investment.

Returns on typical investments

The return on investments varies with the tax treatment of the investment and with the effect of inflation. A 5 per cent return on a term deposit, for example, is not the same as a 5 per cent return on shares. The return on the shares may carry a tax benefit (called a franking credit), and the capital value of the shares may increase over time, whereas the capital value of a term deposit appears to stay the same, but actually decreases at the inflation rate.

Here I will discuss some typical investment returns and how to compare them to your mortgage. For most investment types you can only make estimates, as the returns can be variable from year to year. If you are not familiar with any of the investment types, we will deal with them all in more detail in the next chapter.

Mortgage payments or redraw account

The return on paying extra on your mortgage is the mortgage rate, since you pay no tax on the benefit you gain with extra payments. However, the purchasing power of your money decreases with inflation, and this reduces the benefit of paying off your mortgage. The fact that your house is increasing in value is not relevant here. The amount you owe is a fixed amount, and in terms of what it will buy, it will be worth less in a few years time than it is now. To compensate for inflation, you can subtract the current inflation rate from the mortgage rate to give the real rate of return.

Inflation in Australia is around 2–3 per cent at the time of writing, if we disregard the one-off higher rate for 2001 that was a result of the introduction of the GST.

Term deposits

A term deposit pays a set interest rate for a set time. At the end of your term you have your original capital plus your interest less any tax. The purchasing power of your capital goes down over the years at the inflation rate. So your real return is the interest rate, less the tax, less the inflation rate. At the time of writing, with term deposit rates at around 4 per cent, this could well be negative.

Residential property

The return on renting out property varies with the ratio of the cost of the property to the rent charged. We will look at rental returns in more detail a little later, but they are not generally all that high. At time of writing, 4 per cent to 6 per cent before tax is about average. The value of your property should increase over time, at least at the inflation rate even after the capital gains tax (CGT) is paid. If you are comparing this type of investment, calculate your return and subtract the tax owing, but don't adjust for inflation. You may need the CGT booklet from the Australian Tax Office (ATO) to work out the CGT owing.

Property trusts

Property trusts usually pay around 7 per cent to 9 per cent. Some of your income is tax-deferred, so you will not pay tax on this portion, but you will pay CGT on this when you sell. The value of your property trust shares or units should increase at the inflation rate or higher. For property trust investments, your return is the dividend, less the tax you pay on the taxable portion.

Shares

The return on shares is the dividend, plus any attached franking credit, plus the capital gain on your shares if you hold them for some time, less any tax you pay. Franking credit is just the amount of tax that the company has already paid on your dividend. The amount of franking credit will be shown on your dividend statement. The money is paid directly to the tax department, not to you. The franking credit will reduce the amount of tax you owe. You have effectively already paid this tax. If your franking credit at the end of the year is higher than the tax you owe, the ATO will refund the difference.

If your dividend is fully franked, the franking credit can be calculated as $\frac{3}{7}$ of the dividend, and added on to your net dividend amount to give the total dividend return. If your dividend is partially franked, calculate the franking credit as before, then multiply it by the franking percentage.

For a $70 dividend, the franking credit will be $30. The total of the dividend and the franking credit is taxable, so add these together to give $100 taxable income. For a 50 per cent franked dividend, the franking credit is worth 50 per cent of the $30, which is $15, so your total dividend is $85.

This gives the grossed-up return on your shares. To calculate your after-tax return you now subtract tax at your marginal rate. The share price should go up at least with inflation if you buy blue-chip shares or listed share trusts, so you don't need to compensate for inflation. You may even want to add 2–3 per cent to the return as the sharemarket does increase at a rate higher than inflation over the long term.

Investing in shares may give you a better return than paying off your mortgage provided you choose carefully and don't lose your money gambling on speculative stocks. This is particularly so if you can buy the shares in the name of a low-income partner.

Managed investments

Managed investment returns are usually quoted as the dividend paid to you plus the gain in the price of the units. So the capital gain on the assets of the fund is part of the quoted return. You will need to subtract tax from the dividend, and also allow for inflation, as the capital growth is built into the unit price.

Superannuation

You can contribute your own after-tax money to super or have your employer contribute to super for you. The second case is covered under salary sacrifice below.

The returns given for superannuation funds are the total of the interest or dividends the fund earns, less the 15 per cent tax that the fund pays, and any capital appreciation on the assets. So you will not need to subtract tax from the quoted return. However, as the return includes capital appreciation, you will need to adjust for inflation.

You will also pay tax on the super money when it is paid to you on retirement. This may be in the form of lump sum tax of 16.5 per cent if you take your super as a lump sum, or income tax if you take it as an income stream. The income tax is also around 16.5 per cent for most people, using an income tax rate of 31.5 per cent, less a 15 per cent rebate that most superannuation sourced income attracts. The part of your return that is your own after-tax contributions is tax free, as is the first $100 000 or so of the remainder of your benefit. If your super payout (excluding any after-tax contributions you made) exceeds the reasonable benefit limit (RBL), around $507 000 at the time of writing, then the tax rate is much higher.

This tax on the benefit makes superannuation difficult to compare with other investments. If you reduce the return by

16.5 per cent to allow for this, you will not be strictly accurate. Money compounding at a higher rate for several years then taxed at 16.5 per cent will give a higher value than if the tax was paid each year. However, the difference is not large and subtracting around 15 per cent or so from your super fund return will allow for the tax and give you a reasonable estimate of the real eventual return.

Salary sacrifice

Employer contributions to super are taxed at 15 per cent when they enter the fund. If you are on a high income (over $85 000 including the value of your employer super), your employer contributions may be subject to the superannuation surcharge, and the tax can be as high as 30 per cent.

However, this is still usually less tax than you would pay if your employer paid the money to you directly and you paid income tax on it.

This is the basis for salary sacrifice, where your employer pays part of your salary into your super fund as an employer contribution, rather than paying it directly to you. For every $1000 your employer pays you, you take home $685 if you are on the 31.5 per cent tax rate and $515 if you are on the top tax rate of 48.5 per cent. If your employer pays this $1000 to the super fund, instead of to you, the fund pays 15 per cent tax, leaving $850 for investment. Having $850 compounding in the super fund is usually better than paying the $685 (or the $515) off your mortgage.

For the normal-rate taxpayer (31.5 per cent), the difference between salary sacrifice and investing yourself or paying off your mortgage is quite small, due to the tax when you take the super benefit. If you are a high-income earner in the top tax bracket, however, salary sacrifice is usually the best option for your savings, particularly if your income is below the superannuation surcharge range. But do keep a check on how much super you are accumulating. If you are likely to retire with an amount above the RBL, then putting more money into super is not a tax-effective way to save, as the extra tax when you take the benefit can be quite high.

Also consider the fact that you are locking your money away until you reach a retirement age set by legislation. You cannot choose to retire early on your super no matter how much you have accumulated.

Additional benefits of redraw

There are additional benefits of a mortgage redraw account as well as the higher likely return on your money. Keep these in mind when you choose between an offset account on your mortgage and other investments.

The redraw account gives you immediate access to your money, although there is usually a minimum withdrawal amount and sometimes a fee. A salary account gives you instant access with no fee. A term deposit can usually be accessed before maturity, but there is always an interest penalty for doing this. You can sell shares on reasonably short notice, but you will pay brokerage and you will have to accept the current share price if you need your money in a hurry, which could mean taking a loss. Property can take months to sell. You cannot access the super at all until you retire.

The interest on the redraw account is not actually income, so the extra can't put you into the super surcharge range or affect your family tax benefits.

The redraw account return is reasonably predictable over the years. Mortgage rates do change over time, but this is usually quite slow and not as variable as changes in share prices or super fund returns.

Borrowing to invest

We talked earlier about home equity loans that you can use for other purposes, mainly investment. You may have seen advertisements encouraging you to borrow money on the security of your home to buy a car or a boat, take a holiday, buy a rental property, or invest in the sharemarket.

Borrowing money for cars and holidays is covered later in this book (see p 158) when we work out how we are going to maintain our lifestyle and still have money over to fast-track our mortgage.

Why do some people borrow money against the equity in their home to buy other investments, such as shares or rental property? Why is it better for you to pay off your mortgage when savvy investors are taking out new mortgages and using the money to invest? Why bother to pay off your mortgage at all if you are better off borrowing the money to invest elsewhere?

Many people who borrow to invest pay interest only on their loan and never even try to pay back the principal. This may seem rather hair-raising to you if you are used to the concept that one's ultimate goal in life is to be debt free.

The answer to this apparent paradox lies with the people who make the taxation laws.

When you pay interest on your mortgage, it is not tax deductible. If you borrow money using your house as security and use the money to invest in rental property, managed funds or the sharemarket, the interest on the loan can be claimed as a tax deduction.

The ATO looks at the purpose of the loan, not the details of how you arrange your affairs. Here is an example to illustrate this.

Tax example

Suppose you have $200 000 sitting in a bank account and you want to buy a house worth $200 000 and also put $100 000 into the sharemarket. You first option is to put $100 000 deposit on the house, borrow the other $100 000 and put $100 000 into the sharemarket. The interest on the loan is not tax deductible because the purpose of the loan is to buy the house.

Now suppose you buy the house outright using all of your $200 000, then borrow $100 000 using your home as security and invest this in the sharemarket. Now the interest is a tax deduction. The purpose of the loan was investment.

Tax law is constantly changing. Always check the current rules with your tax adviser if you are considering borrowing money to invest.

Gearing

Borrowing money for investment is called gearing. You make all the profit on the investment (above your interest costs) for little or no outlay of your own money. You can make most of the profits on owning $100 000 worth of shares without ever having $100 000 of your own to invest.

If the interest you pay is higher than your investment income, so you actually make a loss, and you are relying on capital appreciation of the shares or property to eventually make a profit, then you can claim the loss from your normal income as a tax deduction (at the time of writing). This is called negative gearing and I will explain how it works in more detail in Chapter 6.

If you have an equity mortgage on your home and are using the money for investment, or if your mortgage is to buy an investment property, then you may well be better off paying interest only on the loan and not paying back any principal at all. Certainly it is pointless fast-tracking this type of mortgage.

If you borrow money to invest, then the overall return on your investments must be greater than the loan interest rate. Otherwise you are losing money. If you are claiming the interest payments as a tax deduction, then the total investment return must be higher than the mortgage rate before tax. This is much easier to achieve than an after-tax return greater than the mortgage rate.

Borrowing example

Here is an example of why borrowing to invest can work. Suppose you have a home equity loan for $100 000 at 7.5 per cent and you use the money to buy shares in a property trust paying a 9 per cent dividend. We use a 7.5 per cent rate, as the interest is generally slightly higher for this type of loan than for a standard mortgage. You pay $7500 per year in interest, and receive $9000 per year in dividends. You gain $1500 per year before tax. You pay tax on the $9000, claim the $7500 as a tax deduction, and even on the top tax rate, you are over $750 a year better off. You gain this $750 with no outlay at all of your own money. It may not sound a lot, but it is free. And the value of your property trust shares may go up over time, so you get some capital gain as well. In this instance, the more you borrow, the more you gain.

If the investment is paying less than 7.5 per cent in dividends and capital gain, then you are losing money, and it is pointless for you to borrow money for that particular investment.

To borrow money against the equity in your home for investment purposes and claim the interest as a tax deduction, you need to already have a reasonable equity in your home, so you can take out a separate loan for investment purposes. Remember the purpose of the loan must be for investment. It isn't good enough to tell the ATO that you have $10 000 in investments that you could have used to pay off your home loan, therefore $10 000 of your loan is for investment purposes and that proportion of your loan interest is deductible. This may seem perfectly logical to you, but the ATO will not allow you to claim the deduction.

Here is one last example to illustrate how fine-tuning the structure of home and investment loans can benefit you.

Inheritance example

Imagine you are an ordinary family with a home worth around $150 000 and $100 000 owing on a mortgage at 7 per cent. An aunt of yours dies and leaves you $100 000.

Your first option is to continue to pay off your loan in the usual way, and put the $100 000 in an investment at 9 per cent. Your second option is to pay the whole amount off your mortgage. The third option is to pay off the mortgage, then reborrow the amount to invest. The interest rate for this type of loan is usually a little higher. I have used 7.5 per cent, and I have used a tax rate of 31.5 per cent including Medicare levy.

Your annual accounts for the three different options are set out in Table 3.8.

Table 3.8 Comparing loan payout with investment

	Invest the money $	Pay off the loan $	Restructure the loan $
Interest on loan	-7000	nil	-7500
Tax deduction	nil	nil	2362
Interest on investment	9000	nil	9000
Tax on investment	-2835	nil	-2835
Net gain or outgo	-835	nil	1027

The first option is costing you $835 a year compared to paying off the home loan. With the second option, you no longer pay any interest or gain any income. With the third option you are $1027 better off. This only works where the money is invested at a higher rate (before tax) than the mortgage rate.

Remember this is for people who like to squeeze everything they can out of their money. Using the extra money to pay off the mortgage was better than investing it without restructuring the loan, and this works for small amounts as well as large. It is also risk-free. If the investment return dropped, or the investment failed altogether, you may be sorry you had not just paid off the mortgage.

Investment property loans

There are two approaches to borrowing money to buy residential rental property. You can buy a property and pay it off just like you would your own home, or you can treat it as an investment just like we did in the investment examples above and pay interest only on the loan for the time that you own the property.

There are tens of thousands of Australians who own residential rental property and we will talk about fast-tracking this type of mortgage.

Suppose you were paying $1000 a month off your home loan. When you finish paying it off, you will have that amount available to pay off an investment property loan. But you will also have rent coming in. Suppose the net rent, after you pay management fees, council rates and property maintenance, is $600 a month. You can add this to your payment each month. This would reduce the term for a mortgage of $100 000 at 7 per cent from 13 years ($1000 a month repayment) to around six or seven years ($1600 a month repayment).

When you have paid off one house, you can use your $1600 a month to save the deposit for your next house. When you have bought the second house, you will have your $1600 a month, plus another $600 rent from the second house, giving you $2200 to use as your mortgage payment. Each house can be paid off more rapidly than the one before and you could easily retire with three or four rental properties. This would depend on the price of houses in your area, and the rent to capital cost ratio.

The rent from three or four properties would probably give you enough income to retire on, or you could sell the houses and put the money in investments with a higher income return. Buying residential rental property like this will not give you a high investment return, but it is safe, most people understand it, and lots of people do it. Many people enjoy doing up houses or just enjoy being landlords and you may make a large capital gain.

The second approach is to borrow as much as you can of the cost of the home on an interest only loan, leaving your own funds to invest elsewhere. You will still get the same capital gain when you sell, and if your own funds are returning a before-tax rate of more than the mortgage rate, then you are gaining.

You can borrow all of the cost of the investment home, and often the purchase costs as well if you fully own your own home, or if your current mortgage is only a small proportion of the value of your home. The bank will take both homes as security for the loan, so you can borrow up to 80 per cent of the combined value of the rental home and your home. This allows you to buy rental property without spending any of your own funds at all.

Under current tax law at time of writing, you can claim any ongoing loss you make on the difference between the amount you pay in interest and costs and the net amount you receive in rent against your other income. This gives you a tax rebate that will help to fund the ongoing costs of the rental property. If you can invest your other funds at a higher rate than the mortgage rate, you will also be gaining over paying your own funds off the loan. This is a situation where it is not better to fast-track the mortgage.

Taking this one step further, if you have a partner in a lower tax bracket, you can gain more by having your funds invested in your partner's name, and the investment house in yours. So you get the higher tax deduction on the loss, and your partner pays less tax on the income from other investments.

Rental property example

If you buy a house for around $200 000, as an example, you could expect to rent it for about $200 to $250 a week. You would need to pay rates, house insurance, landlord's insurance, management fees and maintenance. Even at $250 a week rent, this would give you a net return on your money of less than $200 a week. Allow for the house to be empty for a couple of weeks a year and your income reduces to about $180 a week. These figures are just estimates to give you an idea of a typical return on rental property.

This $180 net per week is a return of only about 4.5 per cent on the $200 000 you invested. If your house was rented at only $200 a week, this would reduce to less than 3.5 per cent. If you are borrowing money at 7 per cent, then you need a capital gain of at least 2.5 per cent to 3.5 per cent to break even, more to turn a profit. In fact, you are relying on a capital gain to make a profit at all. You also have to cover the considerable costs of buying and selling the property, including stamp duty, estate agent's fees and loan set-up fees. As well as this, you have the hassles of property maintenance, you may have problem tenants who leave without paying the rent, and you have the effort of buying and selling the house. Property usually does go up in price at a higher rate than inflation, and can sometimes go up very quickly in a short time (a boom), so most property investors do make money, but the return while you own the house is not that great.

Why invest in property

Why do so many people have investment houses? I think the answer lies back in history. The current property investors (the baby boomer generation) left school or graduated from university in the late 1960s and early 1970s when house prices were ludicrously low compared to today. On the other hand, so were wages. In those days $20 000 would buy you a reasonable house in a reasonable suburb, but then $10 000 was a good wage. Through the late 1970s and the 1980s we had an inflation rampage that made house prices skyrocket as land costs rose and building became more and more expensive with rising wages. The baby boomers easily paid off their original $15 000 mortgages from their rapidly rising pay packets and looked for somewhere to invest their spare cash.

It was all very well having a house worth a heap more than you paid for it, but if you sold it and collected the profit, you would have to buy an equally expensive house because you had to have somewhere to live. The obvious answer was to buy a second house that you could sell when the price went up. The sharemarket was attractive too, particularly in the mid-1980s, but in 1987 the share market crashed in a big way. The baby boomers who had invested in shares got their fingers burned and went back to residential property, which was still going up. Houses didn't lose half their value overnight the way that shares did. Property went up and up. Your $20 000 house was now worth $100 000. Your $20 000 worth of shares in Bond Corporation (for example) was now worth nothing.

There is still money to be made buying residential real estate and property investors claim that property returns beat sharemarket returns.

Many people will happily borrow money for property investment when they would never, ever consider borrowing money to buy shares. You may not get all of your money back if you have to sell a house in a hurry, but you will almost always get back enough to pay back the loan, and you can never lose the lot as you can with shares.

We will talk more about investment types in Chapter 6, but for now, if you buy investment property, you can make the choice whether you fast-track the mortgage, pay interest only, or stay somewhere in the middle and put some of your funds into other investments.

Managing money 4

Before we talk about finding the extra for your mortgage payment, we'll talk about managing money and how this will help you maximise the benefits of offset for your loan option.

Back in the first chapter I showed you how to allocate your income to living expenses, fixed costs, car payments or car savings, emergency costs and mortgage payment.

Most personal cash management systems work on the principal of allocating part of your income to various uses in this way, but you don't have to have a formal system for this idea to work. If you do like formal systems I will show you a basic one that you can then make as detailed and complex as you like. There are also some computer-based ones available.

Each fortnight or month you receive a certain amount of money on a regular basis and perhaps some extra money for part-time work, bank interest, holiday loading or share dividends. Each fortnight or month you pay out for food, clothes and petrol; other consumer items like furniture or CDs; fixed costs such as insurance, car repayments, rent or mortgage payments; and emergency costs like medical bills or unexpected car repairs. Somehow you need to ensure that the amount you get in is greater than or at least equal to the amount that you spend. Otherwise you will get further and further into debt.

While the fixed costs and mortgage and rent costs are finite and easily calculated for the year, at least approximately, the scope for spending on consumer items is limitless. How do you know how much you can spend now and still have enough to cover the council rates when they are due later in the year?

There are four aspects to managing money that will help you to keep control of what you spend, and always have enough to pay bills as they come due:

1. Keep absolute track of all your bank accounts and investments. Always know exactly how much you have and where it is.
2. Set aside a sufficient amount each pay to cover long-term (retirement) savings, mortgage or rent, fixed costs, emergency costs and vehicle replacement costs.
3. The remainder is yours for living expenses. Never exceed this amount.
4. If you use a credit card for purchases, keep track of what you owe and never buy more than you can easily pay off when the statement arrives.

Track your bank accounts

Some people always keep track of their bank account balances, others don't. It is essential to do this if you are fast-tracking your mortgage because it will help you to control what you spend, and to see where your money is going.

There are three types of bank accounts that it is imperative for everyone to keep track of. The first is any account that has a chequebook, the second is any account that you use for automatic payments and the third is a credit card. You cannot normally overdraw a keycard (debit card) account as the ATM, EFTPOS machine or bank teller will not allow you to overdraw. But if you have payments automatically deducted, you may not have enough to cover the payment, and the bank may charge you a fee of around $25 if your account becomes overdrawn. You can overdraw a cheque account easily by writing a cheque when you don't have enough left in your account. You can rack up huge amounts on a credit card if you have only a vague idea of what you have spent already.

Most people track their bank accounts, but not their credit card, although this is just as easy to do.

Tracking a bank account

If you don't already keep track of all your accounts, then start today. Buy an accounting notebook with five columns, and set it up like the example in Table 4.1. You can use a spreadsheet for this if you want to. Label your columns as I have.

Find your current balances from your bank or an ATM or from the Internet if you have an Internet banking facility. Write this balance on the first line. For the balance on the next line, use the balance from the first line, less any withdrawals you have made, plus any deposits.

Every time you take out cash from an ATM, pay for something using EFTPOS, buy something using your credit card, have payments automatically deducted, or transfer money between accounts, then write the transaction in your book. Every time you get a payslip, bank a cheque or have interest or dividends paid into your account, write the amount in and recalculate the balance.

Table 4.1 Example bank account

Date	Item	Income	Outgo	Balance
2-Nov-01	Brought forward			2000.00
4-Nov-01	Salary in	1200.00		3200.00
4-Nov-01	Mortgage		1050.00	2150.00
5-Nov-01	Cash from ATM		150.00	2000.00
8-Nov-01	Dividend from Telstra	60.00		2060.00

If you are using Internet banking, check your balance regularly and look up any bank fees or government debit tax (GDT) that you have paid. Transfer these to your account book.

Tracking a credit card

Do the same with your credit card, so you keep track of what you owe. A lot of people keep track of their bank accounts, but not their credit cards. Treat your card like a bank account, and think of the amount you owe on your card as part of your overall bank balance. That way you are less likely to find at the end of the month that you don't have enough cash to pay the full balance. A credit card tracking system is shown in Table 4.2.

If you can't cope with the negative numbers, then change the heading of the last column to **Owing**, add the amount you spend on the card, and subtract the payments, so the balance is always positive. Just remember, though, that this is money you owe, not money you own. If you are using a spreadsheet, stick with the negatives, or you may find you are adding your credit card balance to your other account totals instead of subtracting it.

Spreadsheet tip

If you are running this on a spreadsheet, then put the brought forward balance in the income column as well as the balance column on the first line. This will allow you to set up a total line at the bottom of your worksheet with a total of all income amounts less all outgo amounts to give your current balance at a fixed place on the page. If you put all your accounts as separate pages on the same worksheet, you can then link this balance to another page with a summary of all your accounts. As you add entries, just insert lines above the total line. Here is the spreadsheet version of the example account. The balance column formula is just the balance on the line above, plus the income on the current line, less the outgo on the current line.

Example bank account spreadsheet

Date	Item	Income	Outgo	Balance
2-Nov-01	Brought forward	2000.00		2000.00
4-Nov-01	Salary in	1200.00		3200.00
4-Nov-01	Mortgage		1050.00	2150.00
5-Nov-01	Cash from ATM		150.00	2000.00
8-Nov-01	Dividend from Telstra	60.00		2060.00
	Insert new lines here as needed			
	Total of account			**2060.00**

Table 4.2 Example credit card account

Date	Item	Income	Outgo	Balance
1-Nov-01	Brought forward			-60.00
1-Nov-01	Insurance		180.00	-240.00
3-Nov-01	Just Jeans—Jeans for Sue		40.00	-280.00
5-Nov-01	Harvey Norman—Heater		30.00	-310.00
8-Nov-01	Bunnings—Paint		50.00	-360.00
14-Nov-01	Payment to 7 Nov 01	310.00		-50.00
18-Nov-01	K-Mart—CD		20.00	-70.00

Internet banking

If you have access to the Internet, you can normally arrange to have online access to your bank accounts. You can look up your current account balances and your recent transactions and you can transfer money between accounts and pay bills online. This makes keeping track of bank balances really easy.

Internet banking will normally give you an up-to-date balance for a keycard account. For a credit card account it may take a day or two for the transaction to reach your statement.

You may be able to have your home loan account or redraw account linked so you can make extra payments online whenever you like. You will also have instant access to your home loan balance, and the value of your offset each month.

Tracking your assets

You will need to list your assets for the bank when you apply for a loan. You will also want to keep track of your assets so you know your financial position.

For the bank, you will need a list of:

- your bank account balances;
- your credit card balances;
- term deposits;
- any shares or managed investments that you own;
- the value of your vehicle;
- any amount owing on your vehicle;
- any other houses that you own;
- any other mortgages;
- any other loans;
- any tax amounts owing or refunds due;
- your superannuation;
- the estimated value your furniture and household goods; and
- any other assets such as jewellery.

For your own records, you will not need to include some of the assets you listed for the bank when you apply for a loan, although you can if you want to, and many personal accounting books recommend this.

Personally I find it a bit pointless to include the value of your furniture, appliances, jewellery and other personal items in your list of assets for personal accounting purposes. These will only be relevant if you are considering selling everything you own to move abroad, are splitting with your partner, are declaring yourself bankrupt, or if you have one foot in the grave and are considering your children's inheritance. The amount you could sell these items for is variable anyway and probably not a lot compared with what you paid. If you bought the jewellery for investment and know its current cash value, well maybe then you could include it.

The important assets to keep track of on a regular basis for managing money are:

- your bank balances;
- your credit card balances;
- any loans excluding vehicle and home loans; and
- any liquid investments you have.

Liquid investments are investments that you could convert to cash within a week or two. This includes shares, managed funds and term deposits. The bank will usually allow you access to term deposits early, but you will pay an interest penalty. The total value of these assets represents your available liquid funds.

Don't subtract your vehicle or home loans at this point, or you may have a depressingly huge negative balance. This negative balance will only be meaningful if you add the value of your car and your home, neither of which you can readily convert to cash.

Your house, your vehicle, your superannuation and money that other people owe you are not available funds. They are non-liquid or fixed assets. You can keep track of these separately if you want to.

If someone owes you money, or you are expecting a tax refund, keep track of this as a non-liquid asset. You may never be paid, and you can't spend a tax return until you receive it.

If you owe money on your car, keep track of the current insured value and the amount you still owe. If you fully own your car, you may prefer to leave it out of the calculations altogether. The only times the value will matter is if it is written off and you collect the insurance money, or if you are selling it or trading it in.

If you have a home loan, then note the purchase price of

your home and the amount you still owe. You can use the current market value of your home less selling costs if you want to, but this is not always easy to assess.

If you have any other property, keep track of this separately as a non-liquid asset. You can sell property, but it may be a long time before you actually get the money. The value for accounting purposes is the amount you paid (or what you consider is the current market value less selling costs), less the amount of any mortgage on the property. This is a non-liquid asset, but is still part of your overall investments, so do include it somewhere on your asset list.

Keep track of the value of your superannuation just for interest. You will receive a statement each year, and this is really all the record you need.

If you enjoy counting your hoarded gold and want to list everything you own and subtract everything you owe just once in a while, then by all means do this. But don't bother with furniture, boats, artwork or jewellery unless you bought them for investment purposes. The total will become meaningless.

If you keep your bank balances on a computer spreadsheet, then have an extra page listing all your account balances, the total balance, and the value of any investments you have. Otherwise just add this up once in a while and write it at the back of your account book. Table 4.3 is an example spreadsheet showing assets.

You will notice I have not added the total of the liquid assets to the total of the fixed assets and the super. You can do this if you want to, but it is adding apples and oranges to some extent. You may want to total your liquid assets, any investment property you own and your super if you would like an estimate of the amount that you currently have

Table 4.3 Asset summary worksheet

Summary of assets			
Bank accounts			
Keycard	2060		
Cheque	250		
Savings	4500		
Redraw	6000		
Bankcard	–540		
Total		**12 270**	
Investments at cost			
Telstra shares	2400		
Caltex shares	600		
Hunter Hall Managed Fund	1850		
Total		**4 850**	
Total liquid assets			**17 120**
Vehicles			
Insured value of Fred's car	10 500		
Owing on HP	–4500		
Value of Sue's car	2000		
Net value of vehicles		**8 000**	
Value of home			
Purchase price	180 000		
Owing on mortgage	–130 000		
Equity in home		**50 000**	
Total fixed assets			**58 000**
Superannuation			
Fred's super at 30 June 01	18 000		
Sue's super at 30 June 01	4000		
Total super		**22 000**	

available for your retirement. If you are 50, then this might be useful. If you are 25, forget it.

Valuing investments

Investments need to be valued on a consistent basis. There are three ways you can value investments. The first way is what you paid for them. The second way is on cashflow, using what you paid less any cash return you have made from dividends or profits on investments sold. The third way is to look up the current value and use this.

If you value your investments at cost, then if you sell an investment you need to subtract from your total the amount that you paid for that investment rather than the amount you sold it for.

If you value your investments on cashflow, you add any investment purchases, and subtract any income and the proceeds of any investments sold. Eventually, the value of your investments could reduce to zero or become negative using this method, so while it may be useful to you to know the cashflow amount, it is not a useful valuation method.

The third method is probably the best method for most purposes. Every month or so look up the current value of any shares or managed investments that you own, and subtract any selling costs, such as brokerage, that you will incur if you sell, and any tax that you would owe. This gives a reasonable estimate of the cash you would have available if you needed it.

Real property (houses and land) is a bit more difficult to value than shares or managed funds. For most purposes you can just use the purchase price of the property as your valuation. If you think the property is worth much more than you paid, or if you have owned it for several years, then by all means use the expected selling price less any selling costs. Your equity in the property is the valuation less any amount that you owe on a mortgage.

Setting aside expenses

Your income has to cover bills, rent or mortgage, cars and transport and buying food and personal items. When we looked at how much you could afford to pay off your mortgage, we talked about setting amounts aside to cover fixed costs, vehicle replacement costs and emergencies, and I showed you how to work out how much you needed to set aside for these costs (see p 20).

Try to allocate around 10 per cent of your take-home pay to long-term savings. You can put this towards your mortgage payment or invest it independently in superannuation or other savings. This amount, saved over a lifetime, will allow you to retire comfortably well off or even wealthy, and tucking away the 10 per cent each payday is easy to calculate and easy to achieve. If you start from your first pay packet, you will never miss the money.

Think about a virtual pigeonhole system for your money. When you get your pay, imagine yourself dividing it up into pigeonholes for storage until needed. Each pay you will put in an amount for each purpose, and when you need to make a payment, the money will be there waiting. If you put $250 into your mortgage pigeonhole each week, then when you come to make the monthly payment, the $1000 is there ready. I will show you several ways of actually setting up these virtual pigeonholes a bit further on.

Think about dividing your money up when you receive your pay into what you need for:

- long-term savings;
- rent or mortgage payment;
- fixed costs like rates and electricity;
- car payment or saving to buy your next car;
- emergency costs; and
- living expenses.

If you work for yourself, or have income from investments, you may also need to set aside money to pay your tax.

Long-term savings

This is the 10 per cent of your take-home pay that we talked about above. Add this to your mortgage payment. This may be all the extra you need to fast-track your mortgage by ten years or more. If you can manage the extra on your mortgage in other ways, you may prefer to put this into superannuation and non-super investments.

If you think there is no way you can have 10 per cent of your income spare, just keep reading. We will cover this later on in the book. We are still working on an ideal system at the moment.

Mortgage or rent

This is quite straightforward. If you pay your mortgage monthly and are paid weekly, divide the mortgage payment by 4.33 and set this amount aside each pay. If you are paid fortnightly, divide the monthly payment by 2.17.

If you pay your mortgage weekly or fortnightly instead of monthly, arrange for the payment to be taken from your account a day or two after you are paid, to allow for late salary payments and differences in public holidays between states. The extra day or two will give you a chance to transfer funds from somewhere else if you need to. You may even be able to have the amount deducted from your pay before you get it.

Fixed costs

Fixed costs (the things you pay every year or every few months) are not normally evenly distributed throughout the year. You may pay your council rates and your car insurance and registration in the same month, then pay no fixed costs at all the following month. If you work out the total of all these costs for the year, then divide by the number of times you are paid, you will know how much of your pay to set aside each payday to cover these costs.

Each pay you put the amount that you calculated into a virtual pigeonhole marked 'fixed costs' and, when a bill arrives, you take out some of the money to pay it. Provided you started with the correct amount in your pigeonhole, you will always have enough to pay the bills. You will need to make minor adjustments each year as costs increase or change, but once the system is set up, it runs itself rather nicely. Goodbye worries about bill payments.

List all your fixed costs like power, water, rates, insurance and vehicle costs and add up the total for a year. Then divide this by the number of times you are paid in a year, for example 26 if you are paid fortnightly. Round this up to the next ten dollars to allow for small annual increases. This is your fixed costs amount that will go into the fixed costs pigeonhole each payday.

Some of these costs, such as health insurance, may be deducted directly from your pay. Just leave these amounts out of your calculations.

You may need a little fine-tuning as you go. If you have a

new fixed cost, a mobile phone for example, you will need to calculate an amount per pay for this and add it to the amount you transfer for fixed costs.

You may need to start the system with some money in this pigeonhole. If you are due to pay the council rates, insurance and vehicle registration next week, then one week's amount is not going to cover it. Work out the largest three bills you pay during the year, add the total of these and start with this amount. You may need to make minor adjustments in the first year if this does not turn out to be enough.

Vehicle replacement costs

Now think about cars. You may have bought your car with borrowed funds, or you may have paid for it directly. Paying cash for cars is a cheaper way to buy them as:

- you may get a discount for cash;
- you will pay more for insurance if your car is on hire purchase; and
- you will be paying interest costs and loan set-up fees if you borrow money.

If you are paying your car off, then it is usually better for you to put any extra you have towards your car loan than towards your home loan. When you have paid the car off (most vehicle loans are for around five years), keep it for another five years and put the amount that you were paying towards your next car. After the five years, you should be able to pay cash for a new car.

If you fully own your vehicle, start setting aside the money for your next one. Cars don't last forever. If you buy a new car every ten years, then divide the cost of a new car by ten, and save this amount each year. Car prices will have risen by then, but your ten-year-old car should still be worth something, and this should cover the price rise. If you buy a car every five years, then divide the cost by five. Your five-year-old car will have some residual value, probably one-third to one-half of what you paid for it. You can take this amount from the new car cost before you do the calculation if you want to, but do allow for price rises.

If the type of car you buy is around $26 000, and you want to replace it every ten years, you will need to save $2600 a year, or $100 per fortnight, towards replacing it. This rough calculation method is fine.

You need to take into account the current age of your car, of course. If your car is already eight years old, you are not going to save enough to replace it within two years unless you put in a lot more than this. You have two choices here. If you have enough available funds, you can set aside part of your funds (eight years' worth of the payment amount you calculated) for your next car, and save the rest over the next two years. Or you can put more each pay into your next car savings, so you save enough to replace your car over two years.

Remember, if you are paying off your vehicle then this amount is just your car loan payment. Work out a per-pay amount for your payment and store this amount. You may prefer buying your car on credit, you may believe leasing a car is the best way to go, or you may have access to a company car. If so, just put aside what you need for hire purchase or lease payments.

Now you have worked out what to save, mentally pigeonhole this amount of your pay into a 'next car' virtual pigeonhole.

Emergency expenses

Allow something for emergency expenses such as failed appliances, medical bills, major car repairs and house repairs. This is more difficult because these expenses are not predictable in the way that fixed costs are.

If you allow $100 per fortnight that you set aside into a virtual 'emergency' pigeonhole, then this should cover most of this type of cost. If your family is prone to major disasters, allow more, if you have sailed through five years with no disasters, allow less.

Tax expenses

If you work for yourself and pay your tax in installments, it is imperative to keep at least a rough track of what you owe and ensure you never spend this amount on something else. If you find that accurately calculating the amount of tax to store is a bit tedious, then work out the proportion of your gross pay that you paid in tax last year and store away the same proportion of every payment you receive this year. If you didn't work for yourself last year, then store away one-quarter to one-third of your income as you receive it.

Looking after living expenses

With all these fixed expenses catered for, what's left in your pay packet is yours to live on. If your hair stands on end at the thought of living on this, you may already be financially overcommitted. We will look at this shortly.

You may want to further subdivide this into housekeeping expenses, household goods, clothes, personal items and anything else you like. You may want to set a portion of it aside for buying large family items, like new furniture. It is a good idea to give each family member a small allowance that they can spend on anything they want. If they don't spend it all, it can be accumulated. Children can put any excess into their own bank account. Adults can take their allowance as needed and keep track of how much they still have available.

Fixed costs like mortgage payments and insurance bills will look after themselves if you set your system up properly, because these are finite and easily predictable payments. This is not so with living expenses. You can, in theory, go on spending money forever on consumer products. You need some way of controlling what you spend so you don't exceed the money you have available to live on.

In these days of credit cards, you can even spend more than the total amount of money you have in the bank. Eventually you will reach a credit limit, but you can have several credit cards from banks and retail stores, provided you always manage to pay the minimum and don't get yourself a bad credit rating.

You are in control of your own finances at this point. No money management system by itself can stop you spending more than you have available unless you physically limit the amount of cash you have in the bank accounts you can access with your keycard, and cut up your credit cards.

Having said that, most people are reasonable money managers by the time they get to buy houses and pay off mortgages. In the next chapter I will give you lots of ideas on reducing the amount you spend on day-to-day living. The important thing is to know how much you have available for living expenses and find some way of sticking to it that works for you. I will show you some ways to do this a little further on.

Pay any extra towards your mortgage

This living expense portion of your money is very important for fast-tracking your mortgage. This is because the only way you will have extra to pay off your mortgage (above the long-term savings amount you set aside) is to have some of this living expense money over.

Living expenses are reasonably constant from week to week, or at least month to month. If you have any cash over at the end of the month, then pay it off your mortgage. Don't spend it just because you have it.

Table 4.4 is an example income allocation for a family with our standard mortgage and a total take-home pay of $1400 per fortnight including the value of any family allowance and tax benefits. This would represent a gross pay of around $42 000 to $45 000 total for both partners, depending how the income was split, less than this if the couple had children and was paid family allowance.

This allocation allows an extra $300 a month mortgage payment (the long-term savings of $140 per fortnight) and

Table 4.4 Allocating your pay

	Per fortnight
Long-term savings	140
Mortgage ($707 per month)	330
Vehicle savings	100
Fixed costs	150
Emergency	100
Living expenses	580
Total	**1400**

$100 a fortnight saved towards the next vehicle. This $100 could be put into a redraw account until it was needed, accelerating the mortgage by a further two years.

Use your credit card carefully

Here are some frightening statistics on credit cards that you may not know or may not have thought about:

- Collectively we Australians owe around $18 billion on our bank-issued credit cards at time of writing. This works out to almost $1900 for each account, and nearly $1000 for every person living in Australia. Some of this is paid off each month when the statement comes, but at least $10 billion of it is carried forward each month and the credit card providers earn around $1.5 billion a year in interest. That's an average of nearly $200 per card per year.
- Every year hundreds of Australians, many (but not all) of them young people, go bankrupt because they have racked up credit card balances that they can never pay off. Bankruptcy is not something to be taken lightly.
- If you owe $5000 on your credit card, you never charge anything else to your card, and you pay off the minimum amount each month (usually 2.5 per cent of the total with a minimum of $25), then it will take you seventeen years to pay off the balance and you will have paid around $5000 in interest over this time. Everything on your card will have cost you twice what you paid for it.

We will talk a bit more about consumer debt in the next chapter. From a managing money aspect, the important thing is to use your credit card sensibly. It is handy to charge purchases rather than paying cash, and using a credit card rather than a debit card can save on bank transaction fees. Credit cards also allow you to keep as much as possible in offset accounts.

If you keep track of the balance on your card, you should be able to keep within an amount that you can pay off before you owe interest on it. Have the type of card with the 55 days interest-free feature, rather than the type where you pay interest from day one.

Use your credit card for your convenience and to save you money, not to make profits for the banks.

If you don't think you can manage this

You may look at your costs and your current mortgage payments and living expenses and think putting away 10 per cent of your pay for long-term savings is impossible. You may already be so overcommitted on your mortgage and car payments that you are actually going backwards and getting further and further into debt. You may own your current car but think there is no way you could set aside anything like the amount I suggest towards buying a new one. Okay, let's take a look at this.

First, leave out the long-term savings and the car savings (but not any current car loan payments you make) and work it out again. If you can manage now, then work towards putting aside these extra amounts slowly. Read through Chapter 5 on finding the extra, and sit down with your family and work out some ways you could save more. Start by putting 1 per cent of your income aside as long-term savings and add this to your mortgage payment. After a month, increase it to 2 per cent by cutting down somewhere else. When you reach 10 per cent, start putting money aside to replace your car some time in the future. The values I gave were for buying new cars every ten years or so. If you are happy with less than this, then you will not need as much.

If you are currently in debt on a credit card or on vehicle finance, then use any extra you save to pay these debts first.

If you are still going backwards after you leave out the long-term savings and the car savings, then you need to look at your lifestyle. Read through Chapter 5 and think of areas you can cut down on costs. The bottom line is, you need enough to pay your rent or mortgage, to pay essential fixed costs (you can cancel the non-essential ones), to cover transport to and from work, to have food on the table and enough clothes and blankets that you don't get cold in winter.

If no amount of cutting costs is going to allow you to have enough to get out of debt, then you are probably seriously over-committed. If you are leasing or paying off an expensive car, you may need to sell it or send it back and buy a cheaper car. You may even need to sell your home and buy a cheaper one or rent for a while. If you are hopelessly in debt, seek help from a church or community-based debt counsellor. You will find them helpful and sympathetic and they will help you approach your creditors and arrange for an extension of time or a lower repayment.

Keeping track

When your pay comes into your account, how on earth are you going to remember how much of the total is for what purpose? You may not have spent all of last week's living expenses. How much is left? How much of your money is to go towards your new car? It is easy to lose track of how long you have been saving.

You need some way of knowing how much of your total balance is assigned to what purpose and for this you will need some way of mentally or physically dividing up your money so you can keep track of it.

Separate bank accounts

The easiest way to do this is to have a separate bank account for each purpose. Have your pay put into your living expenses account, then transfer your set amounts out to separate bank accounts for long-term savings, mortgage or rent, fixed costs, your next car, and your emergency savings.

If you can manage this many bank accounts then great, this is the easiest way to manage money. It requires about half an hour's work each year just to recalculate the amounts you need to transfer.

It is easy to be a little more economic with bank accounts than this. You can pay your long-term savings directly into your mortgage redraw account. You can pay your mortgage weekly or fortnightly when your pay comes in, so you don't need to transfer it to a separate account. You can pay your next car money directly into a redraw account on your mortgage, as it may be several years before you need it. You can combine the fixed expenses account with the emergency money, but you will need to keep some sort of track of what you take out to cover emergencies, as this could easily add up to more than you are putting in, leaving you short of funds to pay your bills.

If you are allowed several salary accounts on your mortgage, then this method is great. When your pay comes in, just transfer the amounts you calculated to your other accounts. The amount left in your living expenses account is yours to spend. Conversely, you may want to transfer your living expense amount out to another account, and leave all the other amounts in the account your salary is paid into.

As a minimum, try to physically separate your living expense money from the rest of your funds, and keep your credit card under control. Provided you worked out your car money reasonably accurately and you don't spend more on emergencies than you allowed for, then the rest of your money should look after itself in the one account.

Suppose you keep a separate account for living expenses as I have suggested and when your next pay arrives you still have some left. Can you safely transfer this amount to your mortgage, or should you leave it in your account in case you spend more next fortnight or need to buy a large item? To get around this problem, set a maximum amount that you think you need in reserve. This may be four times your usual living expenses or twice your normal pay, or some amount that you are comfortable will cover pay-to-pay differences in your living expenses. If your account exceeds this just before your pay comes in, then pay the excess off your mortgage or transfer it to your redraw account.

Virtual bank accounts

If you are allowed only one salary account or if you pay fees on your bank accounts, you can work with one account and separate the amounts yourself using a 13-column account book or a computer spreadsheet. This may look complex at first, but it is really quite straightforward, and once you get used to it, it is no more work than keeping track of several separate bank accounts.

What you need to do is to set up virtual bank accounts

inside your single account. Each virtual account needs two columns of your account book or spreadsheet, one for transactions and one for totals. With a 13-column book, you can set up six accounts. With a spreadsheet, you can set up as many as you like. In Table 4.5, I have set up five accounts.

Start by allocating your current funds to the virtual accounts in a brought-forward line. Add all your total values and store the account total in the last column. This should be equal to your current bank account balance.

When your pay comes in, allocate part of it to each account. For this example, the pay is $1500 for the fortnight: $500 of this is put towards the mortgage, $200 goes into the vehicle account, $100 into fixed costs, $100 into emergency and the remaining $600 is allocated to living expenses.

When you withdraw money for any reason, put it in as a negative transaction in its appropriate account. In the example, we pay a power account of $100, and take out $200 cash for groceries. We then pay $1000 on the mortgage, and take out a further $200 living expense money.

The next row is the pay coming in for the following fortnight. Allocate it the same way. The final line is where we pay the bankcard balance for the month. Of this, $200 was used to pay insurance, so this goes into the fixed costs. We had a car repair of $100 and we bought $200 worth of clothes. Keep track of your credit card balance separately, so you always know how much you owe, and what you spent it on.

Work out each account total as you go, then add all the account totals to give the overall total. This should always be equal to your bank balance. Remember that money coming into your account is positive, and money going out is negative. I have highlighted the transaction amounts in bold, to make the example easier to follow.

Keeping track of your virtual accounts is just as easy as keeping track of separate bank accounts once you have set up your account book or spreadsheet. As a minimum, you can set this up with one virtual account for living expenses and one other virtual account for the remainder of your savings.

The lazy way

If you are a diehard lazy accounting person, and keeping track of virtual bank accounts is not for you, and you can only have one salary account on your mortgage, then as a bare minimum, you can:

- work out your living expenses amount by subtracting the other amounts from your pay;
- keep track of withdrawals from your account and credit card transactions that are for living expenses; and
- make sure the latter never exceeds the former.

You may be better off just transferring your living expense money out to another account that you use for day-to-day purchases and for paying your credit card balance, but you will lose offset.

Living within your means

If you have trouble living within your means, try these ideas:

- calculate a per-week amount for living expenses;
- take this amount out each week in cash from an ATM;
- go straight to the supermarket and buy essential groceries for the week ahead and anything else you know you will need;

Table 4.5 Tracking virtual bank accounts

		Mortgage		Vehicle		Fixed costs		Emergency		Living costs		
Date	**Item**	**In/Out**	**Total**	**In/Out**	**Total**	**In/Out**	**Total**	**In/Out**	**Total**	**In/Out**	**Total**	**Total**
1-Nov-01	Brought forward		500		2000		1000		1000		1500	6000
5-Nov-01	Pay in	**500**	1000	**200**	2200	**100**	1100	**100**	1100	**600**	2100	7500
6-Nov-01	Power account		1000		2200	**−100**	1000		1100		2100	7400
7-Nov-01	Living expenses		1000		2200		1000		1100	**−200**	1900	7200
10-Nov-01	Mortgage paid	**−1000**	0		2200		1000		1100		1900	6200
14-Nov-01	Living expenses		0		2200		1000		1100	**−200**	1700	6000
19-Nov-01	Pay in	**500**	500	**200**	2400	**100**	1100	**100**	1200	**600**	2300	7500
20-Nov-01	Bankcard paid		500		2400	**−200**	900	**−100**	1100	**−200**	2100	7000

- go to the service station and fill your car with petrol, and buy any bus or train tickets you will need for the week;
- give your children their pocket money;
- put enough aside in a separate purse to cover items you can't buy too far ahead, like milk and vegetables;
- the rest is now yours to spend—save some of this if you can;
- leave your credit card at home—if you run out of cash, you can't buy anything else.

You may find that for the first few weeks you run out of money, but you will adjust quite quickly. Most of us buy far more consumer goods than we need.

Managing offset accounts

We have looked at ways to keep track of money. We need to relate this to fast-tracking mortgages by making the most of offset accounts.

Whether you have a redraw facility, a Misa account with an offset lower than the mortgage rate, or a salary account, the aim is the same—to keep as much money as possible at the highest possible offset rate for as long as possible.

If you have any offset account at all, then pay for everything you can with a credit card to increase the time you have money in the offset account. But keep track of the credit card. Paying interest on a high credit card balance will more than cancel out the benefit.

No offset accounts

If you have a budget mortgage with no redraw facility or offset account, then you need to keep any money that you don't want to pay off your mortgage but don't immediately need in a savings account or term deposit earning interest.

Keep the equivalent of around two pay amounts as a minimum balance on your day-to-day account and keep everything else in a savings account. If you want to set up a savings account for each purpose, this should be easy. Most banks have no restrictions on the number of accounts you can open. Long-term savings can be used as direct extra payments on your mortgage.

Redraw only

If you have a redraw facility but no other offset account, then you can put your long-term savings amount and your next vehicle money into the redraw, as you will not need to access this money for a long time. If you pay your own tax annually, put this money in the redraw too. If there is a minimum amount you can put into the redraw, just save the extra in a separate account and transfer it when it reaches the set amount. If there is a fee for withdrawal, then this may be all you can do to take advantage of offset.

If there is no fee for withdrawal, and the minimum withdrawal amount is less than $2000, you will be able to store any tax money here even if you pay your tax quarterly. You may also be able to keep around half of your fixed costs and emergency amounts in your redraw. Just redraw the money when you have a really large bill or a lot of bills together.

Redraw and lower offset Misa

If you have access to a Misa account, with an offset lower than the mortgage rate, put your long-term savings, your next vehicle money and any money stored for tax into the redraw and keep the rest in the Misa account. If there is also a minimum withdrawal amount on your Misa you will need to keep your day-to-day money in a separate account. If you can have more than one Misa account and you want to split your money between bank accounts as I suggested above, then you will need a fixed costs account, an emergency account (or a combination account for these) and an account for your living expenses.

Redraw and full offset Misa

If you have access to a Misa account with a full offset but a minimum withdrawal amount, you can store all your money here except your day-to-day living expenses. You may not want to bother putting money into a redraw account at all, unless you think you will otherwise be tempted to spend it.

If you have your fixed costs money in the Misa account and want to pay a fixed cost that is less than the minimum withdrawal amount, pay it from your living expenses account. Just keep track of any of these fixed expenses you pay and transfer money from your Misa to your living expenses account when the total reaches the minimum withdrawal.

Salary account

If you have a salary account, again you may not want to bother putting money into a redraw facility at all; just leave it in your salary account. You can divide your money between separate salary accounts as I suggested above, or keep track of it in one account, or just keep track of your living expenses. This will depend on the options offered by your bank and your preferences for managing your money.

If you find it difficult to live within your means, you may want to transfer your living expenses to a separate account each payday and use this for cash and to repay the living expense amounts on your credit card. Have your salary and any dividends paid into the salary account, and pay your fixed expenses from this account if you have not set up a separate fixed expense account.

Don't underestimate the value of offset accounts

Offset accounts are very useful things to have when fast-tracking your mortgage. Just because the offset is difficult to see and calculate until you get your statement, don't underestimate the value of it. The balance of your salary account may seem small compared to the value of your loan, but it is working for you day and night increasing the amount you are paying back. Even a small extra amount paid off your loan can make a significant difference to the interest you pay over the life of the loan.

A note on cheque accounts

At the time of writing, any bank account with a cheque book facility attracts government debits tax (GDT). This tax is charged on all withdrawals, not just cheques that you write, and it can amount to a considerable amount of money over a year. It may be phased out in 2005 but, at the time of writing, that is still a while away.

To get around this, don't have a chequebook on your salary account, on the account you use for fixed costs, or on the main account you use for day-to-day cash withdrawals. If you set up all your accounts separately, don't have a chequebook on any of them. Set up a separate cheque account. When you need to write a cheque, transfer as much as you need to the cheque account from the account you would normally use to make the payment. Then write the cheque.

Finding the extra 5

So how are you going to find the extra money you need to fast-track your home loan? You may currently spend everything you have left after your mortgage and expenses are paid. Where on earth are you going to find an extra $300 a month?

If you have two incomes, the extra should be really easy. If this is the case, then put in the easy amount, and then find another extra $300 a month. You will pay off your mortgage in double time.

Saving money and living better for less does not mean living on bread and water, washing up bits of plastic food wrap for re-use, using cut down plastic bleach bottles for vases and walking 20 kilometres to work. Living better for less is a whole new attitude to money and the way that you spend it, and a new way of looking at what you own and why you own it.

There are two ways you can save heaps without changing your lifestyle at all. You can buy the same thing for less, and you can avoid buying things you don't end up using. Then there are lots of minor lifestyle changes that won't have much effect on your enjoyment of life, but may save you a lot of money over time.

In one chapter I can't list every possible hint and tip for saving money, but I can show you how you can change the way you think about money and possessions so you spend less.

It is a strange fact of life, that the more you have, the more you spend. If you don't have much to live on, you will manage to live on it quite well. You will not miss the things you can't afford. However, it is also a fact that needs and wants expand to take every cent of cash that passes through your hands and more besides. However much you spend and own, there are plenty more things for you to buy. And the capitalist system wants it that way, because it maximises profit. Most people don't even think about this and keep buying things until they run out of cash and are hopelessly in debt. If you understand this concept, you can overcome it.

Think before you spend

Every time you pick up an article in a shop, ask yourself:

- Do I need this?
- Will I really use or wear it?
- Can I buy this more cheaply elsewhere?
- Where will I put it when I get it home?

If you do this consciously for two or three weeks, it will become second nature.

You also need to think about the less obvious costs, like using petrol and electricity. Can you combine trips, have two people working in the same room with one heater, or have lower wattage globes in passages?

The best money-saving ideas for you are usually the ones

you think up yourself, for your own situation. You know what you spend your money on, so you know best how to save on costs.

I don't have a magic formula that will provide the extra, but I do have a lot of suggestions on ways you can save. The best formula for success at this is motivation. If you want to find the extra, you will find it easily.

If you find it difficult to live within your means, if you tend to spend money just because it is there, then you need to set up a system where you only have access to your living expense money for day-to-day spending.

Keep the whole thing in perspective

Don't get so obsessed with paying off your mortgage that the quality of life for your family suffers. As an example of what I mean, don't cut out family holidays and outings, then realise when your children reach 16 that they have never swum in the sea or built a sandcastle. Keep the whole thing in perspective. Paying off your mortgage and retiring rich should not be your number one priority. Enjoying life, improving the lives of those around you and leaving the world a better place than you found it should all be above retiring rich on everybody's list. However, the ability to manage your finances, save money and look forward to a secure retirement will enhance your enjoyment of life and reduce the amount of stress and worry you need to cope with.

Saved money is worth more than earned money

Saved money is worth more than earned money. To gain $1 of take-home pay, you need to earn nearly $1.50 if you are on the 31.5 per cent tax rate, and nearly $2 if you are on the top marginal rate. To gain $1 of savings, you need to spend $1 less. Keep this in mind when you think about what you spend.

Here are over twenty ways to help find the extra money to make extra payments on your mortgage. I will list them all first, then deal with each of them in some detail, except the first one, which we have already covered. Some of these overlap a little, and some may not apply to your situation, but if you put them all together, you will save enough to fast-track your mortgage by at least ten years and retire wealthy. You can find the extra $300 a month easily.

- Manage your money efficiently. We have just had a whole chapter on this.
- Earn more money. You can work overtime, get a second job or a second income, or make a hobby pay.
- Put any extra money you get into your mortgage. This includes holiday loading, tax refunds, cash back offers, raffle wins.
- Buy the same thing for less. Take advantage of discounts and shop around.
- Buy a similar or substitute item that costs less. This covers house brands, second-hand and just choosing cheaper alternatives.
- Make your money go further. You can do this by running your household efficiently. Stretch your dollars by using things until they are worn out, and economising on appliance use and resources.
- Share resources. You can swap magazines, services and home produce with friends, family and neighbours.
- Reduce your fixed expenses. You may be able to save on power, insurance and other fixed costs.

- Look after your things. Vehicles and appliances last longer if they are correctly maintained. Umbrellas and jackets are less likely to be lost if they are labelled.
- Minor lifestyle improvements. There is a lot of scope for saving money here. Think of these as improvements rather than changes.
- Rearrange your banking. You can save a surprising amount just by following a few simple strategies.
- Make money from your credit card. Using a credit card can earn you shopping vouchers.
- Reduce your vehicle costs. There are lots of ways to save here.
- Don't move house too often. Moving house involves lots of fixed costs like stamp duty and agent's fees that set you back several thousand dollars.
- Do it yourself. There are lots of things you can do yourself to save money.
- Avoid money-wasting habits. Small changes to when, where and why you shop can save you buying things you don't need.
- Avoid buying things that you don't end up using. Think before you spend.
- Don't bring junk home. Junk is anything you don't eat, wear, use or just enjoy owning. Hoarding junk costs money.
- Clear out your junk. Have a garage sale and put the proceeds towards your mortgage.
- Reduce what you spend on jewellery, ornaments, artwork, collections and craft.
- If your family celebrates Christmas then you may spend a lot at this time of year. There are ways to reduce the cost without reducing the enjoyment.
- Stay out of debt. This is the most important one, and the most difficult for some people.

- Change your attitude to money. If you think about where the money came from, where it goes, and what else you could do with it, you will value it more.

Earn more money

There may be ways that your family can earn extra income. You may be able to work overtime or get a second, evening or weekend job.

Don't let your family life suffer, however. It would be a very sad household indeed, if a parent worked seven days a week every week and there were never any family outings.

You may be able to make a hobby pay, by selling craftwork or plants for example. You may not make much, but every bit helps.

Increasing your skills or qualifications may get you a better rate of pay or a better paying job.

If you are a single income family, the non-working partner may be able to get a part-time job. Two incomes are far more tax effective than one, and this is much more efficient than the main income earner working at a second job.

If you have money invested in a bank account, term deposit or shares, have it invested in the name of the lower income earning partner. You will pay less tax and retain more of your interest and dividends.

Put any extra money into your mortgage

If you get any extra or unexpected income, put it straight towards paying off your mortgage. This money could include:

- bank interest and share dividends;
- overtime pay, holiday loading or Christmas bonuses;

- tax refunds;
- family payments from Centrelink or the ATO;
- cash back offers;
- raffle or lottery wins;
- money you inherit; and
- money from selling items you no longer need.

Buying the same thing for less

If you shop around, you can often buy the same thing for a lower price. Look in the telephone book for possible suppliers and phone around first.

You may be able to get discounts on all sorts of goods and services through clubs, trade unions and other associations. Check before you leave for holidays whether you are entitled to a discount at hotels and restaurants. You may be able to get discounted airfares if you book through a credit union. Some professional associations offer discount stockbroking and legal services. Remember this has to be the cheapest price you can get to be worth taking up.

Dry cleaning is often cheaper if you pay when you take the article in, rather than when you pick it up.

If you own shares in some companies you can buy products at a discount. Coles Myer is the most famous one, but there are other companies that offer discounts. These include David Jones and Pacific Dunlop. You may get discount accommodation from some property or hotel trusts, and many wine companies have special offers and discounts for shareholders. Check that the shareholder discount system is still operating before you buy shares in any of these companies.

Check the brochures that come with your junk mail. Grocery stores often have huge discounts on everyday items that you can stock up on if you have the storage space. If you are not in a hurry for something sold by a discount department store, chances are it will be reduced in price at some time. Stock up on videos, cassettes, socks, and anything else you can usefully buy ahead, when the item is on sale.

Some department and discount stores have special days when everything in the store is cheaper by 10 or 15 per cent. Most stores have after-Christmas and mid-year sales. They don't reduce everything, but they may reduce something that you need.

Buy in bulk if you have the space for storage. Large packets are usually cheaper than small packets. Look out for use-by dates, though. It isn't cheaper if you end up throwing half of the large packet out.

Fruit and vegetables are usually cheaper at weekend growers' markets, but make sure you don't spend more on rides and knick-knacks for your children than you save on the fruit and vegies.

Bread baked in-store is reduced at the end of the day in most supermarkets.

Buy a cheaper substitute

You may be able to save money by buying a cheaper substitute product or by buying an item second-hand.

Choice magazine can help you with decisions on a lot of household items. They test a range of products and give recommendations on which is the best overall value for money. You can subscribe to *Choice*, share a subscription with a friend, or read it in your local library.

Supermarket branded products are often a more expensive brand product with a different label. The supermarket doesn't have its own food factory. The real brand food factory just puts the same food into real brand cans or boxes and supermarket brand cans or boxes. The only difference is that the supermarket brand is usually cheaper.

You can buy most things second-hand for much less than the new price. Swap meets and garage sales are an excellent source of second-hand household goods, and charity stores have near-new clothes for only a few dollars.

If you are prepared to accept a two or three year-old computer, you will pay a fraction of the cost of a new one.

Don't pay for prestige. Don't pay extra to buy a product just because it has a designer brand logo. This applies mainly to clothing and cars. Don't pay extra for a product just because it has a picture of a cartoon character or a pop group, or is heavily advertised.

Keep in mind, though, that buying quality often does pay. Don't automatically buy the cheapest product. Consider the quality as well, and the availability of service and spare parts. A top vacuum cleaner may cost three times as much as a cheap one, but it will last five times as long, and it will do a much better job of cleaning the carpets, so they will last longer too. A front-loading washing machine may cost more initially, but you will use less power and water, less detergent, and your clothes will last longer.

There are also ethical issues involved. Buy Australian made and Australian owned products when the choice is available, and always pay the extra to buy free-range eggs.

Make your money go further

Run a *lean-and-mean* household. There are lots and lots of ways to make money go further. Get your family to sit down together and think up some that work for your lifestyle. Give a reward to the one with the longest list:

Here are a few ideas on the type of savings that you can make here:

- turn off lights and heaters when no one is using them;
- don't run your dishwasher until it is full;
- a large washing load costs about the same to wash as a small load;
- don't throw out sheets, towels or clothes just because you are fed up with them; keep them until they wear out;
- don't replace clothes just because fashions have changed, avoid buying extreme fashion clothes and shoes that will look silly in a year or two's time;
- if an appliance fails, get a quote on repairing it before you replace it.

There are lots of other ideas in some of the other sections. Think in terms of running your household efficiently and the rest will follow.

Share resources

Share resources with family, neighbours and friends. There is a lot of scope for saving money on services by swapping expertise, babysitting, home produce and garden services. Here are some ideas:

- mow the lawns for the old lady across the road in exchange for her feeding your pets when you go on holiday;
- take your neighbour's children to school in exchange for her bringing yours home;

- swap a magazine you subscribe to for one a friend subscribes to; that way you read two magazines for the price of one;
- swap CDs, videos, books and computer games with family and neighbours;
- if you don't have a pool and your neighbour does, offer to clean it occasionally in exchange for your children swimming there; and
- swap excess oranges from your tree for the tomatoes your neighbour grows.

Make friends with people in your area. If you help them, they will help you.

Reducing fixed costs

Fixed costs are bills you pay on some sort of regular basis, such as power, water, insurance and magazine subscriptions. We talked about these in the section on managing money. List all yours and look at places where you could save money. Do you really need the product or service, and is there some way you could reduce the cost?

Insurance costs can vary between companies. Get several quotes when you take out or renew insurance. Some companies will give you a large discount on home and contents insurance if you are prepared to carry an excess of $500 or $1000 instead of the usual $100. If you rarely or never make claims, this may suit you.

Pay accounts as soon as you get them if a discount for prompt payment is offered. If you are paying bills monthly rather than annually you may be paying more than you need to.

Don't subscribe to magazines if no one reads them. What about clubs you no longer go to? Do you really need the newspaper delivered every day?

Look after your things

If you look after things they will last longer and you will pay to replace them less often. We will cover vehicles in another section, but there are lot of other things in your home that benefit from regular maintenance.

Fans and air conditioners work more efficiently and last longer if the filters are kept clean. Hairdryers and heaters need the fluff brushed or vacuumed out of them occasionally. If you keep the coils on the back of your fridge dusted the fridge will last longer and be cheaper to run.

Sewing machines and overlockers need regular oiling, although some very new ones are now maintenance free. They also need to be serviced occasionally.

Bicycles last longer if they are kept clean and oiled and are stored under cover. Car polish will help to keep them free from rust.

Kitchen benchtops will last longer if you use pot stands for hot frypans, mats for teapots, trays for cups and chopping boards for chopping. Kitchen cupboards will last longer if you keep them dry. Fix any plumbing leaks as soon as you notice them.

Home maintenance is cheaper than home repairs. Keep your home painted and your roof leak free. Block up mouse holes. Mice can do an enormous amount of damage to food, clothes and electric wiring. Keep garden sheds locked and engrave all power tools.

Carpets will last longer if you put doormats outside and

inside all external doors. Put small mats over areas subject to extra wear. Don't allow children to run around the house with food or drink. Keep pets outside or in tiled areas. Clean any spills immediately. Vacuum your carpets regularly and steam clean them occasionally.

Label anything that may get lost with your name and phone number. This includes jackets, hats, bags, umbrellas and shoes. Engrave all your valuables, and you will be more likely to get them back if they are stolen.

Improve your lifestyle

There is a lot of scope for saving money on minor lifestyle improvements. We can really only cover a few of them here. Again, get your family together to make up some ideas of your own. Think of them as improvements rather than changes.

Quit smoking

Give up smoking, it's bad for your wealth. This always has to be number one on the list, because you can save so much money. If you spend $50 a week on smoking, then putting this money into your mortgage will save you ten years and $50 000. If you spend more than this, then this amount alone could give you the whole $300 a month extra to fast-track.

Think about the time it took you to earn the money you spend on cigarettes, then picture yourself in the garden on a lovely spring day, with the roses blooming and the birds singing while you sit on the soft green grass with a box of matches burning the money.

For most smokers, quitting is difficult and would not be

considered a minor lifestyle change. However, the benefits in extra cash are worth the effort, and help is available for smokers who want to quit.

Packed lunches

Sending your family to school or work with a packed lunch can save $30 to $50 a week, easily. Even if your family members insist on buying their lunch, you could send a drink with them and save $15 a week on drinks. Buy small cartons of fruit juice, cans of soft drink and small bottles of water from your supermarket, put these in the fridge and send them with a small icepack in a lunch container.

You can refill small bottles of water or soft drink from a larger bottle each day.

Outings

When you go on family outings to adventure parks, shows, zoos, etc. it may be impractical to take all of your food and drink with you because of the weight. But you can take some of it. Taking one can of drink each will save you around $4. Taking a packed lunch could save you around $15. That may not eliminate buying fast food, but it will reduce it significantly without anyone being a packhorse for the whole day.

Fast food

Reduce the amount you spend on eating out and ready prepared meals. If your family goes out to a fast food chain once a week, or if you bring home takeaway meals, you may not be popular with your children if you eliminate this in one fell swoop.

Work on reducing it by half, by having real fast food every

second week. On the alternate weeks, get the children to help you to make home takeaway. Have pizzas, hamburgers, hot dogs, or whatever their favourites are, along with a carton of fruit juice or a large bottle of soft drink that you got on special at the supermarket and a bowl of homemade popcorn. Vary the meals between weeks.

The children may even want to take over the whole cooking on these nights. It is much cheaper to make your own fast food, much better for you, and usually nicer than the real thing. You can even buy a ready made frozen pizza for much less than the takeaway version, or ready crumbed chicken and frozen chips.

Make it a treat. If your family likes eating out rather than at home, try taking your home takeaway to the local park in the summer, or have a barbecue, or make enough for two extra and take your meal to share with grandparents.

Entertainment

Board games, jigsaws, kite flying, walking, bike riding, the beach, television, hiring videos and reading stories are all inexpensive forms of entertainment that the whole family can be involved in.

If you want to see a particular film, hire the video when it is released, or wait for it to come to television. You don't generally have to wait long.

Reduce your gambling

If you play Lotto, or buy raffle tickets on a regular basis, stop and add up what it costs you in a year. Some people spend over $50 a week on Lotto. Dreaming how you would spend the money is fun, but you can dream just as much with one ticket as you can with several, and if you are meant to win, you will anyway. Buy one ticket occasionally and put the rest of your gambling money into your mortgage.

Home computers

Home computers are great. But you need to look at them sensibly, and not buy every new gismo and every new game. If your computer is five years old, but it does everything you want, keep it, however much your children argue.

If your children want the latest and greatest computer games, get them to save their pocket money and buy them for themselves. They will appreciate them more. Or get the children to give a birthday list of the games they want to relatives. Most games are very similar anyway. New ones are often only a slightly rehashed version of a previous game.

Reduce your alcohol consumption

Alcoholic drinks are more expensive than non-alcoholic drinks, partly because they are taxed more heavily. There are lots of interesting non-alcoholic drinks available. Reducing the amount you spend at the liquor store may go a long way to helping you pay off your mortgage. Giving up alcohol may affect your lifestyle a lot; reducing alcohol will only affect it a little.

Rearrange your banking

You may have a free credit card and a transaction-fee-free account with your mortgage. If the bank doesn't offer this, ask and you may get it. Don't underestimate the value of this. You can save a good $200 a year here.

If you do pay transaction fees, keep them to a minimum by taking cash out in larger amounts and putting most of your purchases and your bills on a credit card.

The banks actually have the system set up so that it is cheaper to use a credit card. They get a proportion of the amount you spend from the retailer, and they think that maybe you won't be able to pay off your statement when it comes, so they will get their interest too. Beat the banks at their own game. Put your purchases and bills on your card so you save on fees and earn more on offset accounts, then pay it off in one hit, so they don't get any interest. They will get their fee from the retailer, but this cost is built into the price you pay for goods anyway.

When you use an ATM, choose one belonging to your bank. You may pay a fee of around $1.50 each time you use a different bank's ATM, and this fee is usually payable even if your account is otherwise transaction-fee-free. If you are shopping somewhere where your bank doesn't have an ATM, then pay EFTPOS and take extra cash out.

Government debits tax (GDT) can add up to a lot of money and is a terrible nuisance when arranging your banking. We mentioned this in Chapter 4. You pay GDT on every single withdrawal from any account that has a cheque facility. The amount of GDT varies with the amount of the withdrawal and between states, but it can add up to a lot. Your bank can give you the values for your state or territory.

This tax is with us until 2005, so we need to minimise it. There are two ways that you can reduce the amount you pay. Use both ways. Pay everything you can with a credit card instead of sending a cheque and keep your cheque account separate from your normal bank account.

Most fixed expenses can be paid with a credit card,

including insurance, council rates, power and water. If you are using Internet banking, most of these can also be paid directly online.

Keep a separate cheque account, and don't have a chequebook on the account you use for your normal day-to-day banking. When you need to write a cheque for something you cannot pay for any other way, transfer the money from your usual account into your cheque account at an ATM or via Internet banking, then write the cheque.

Make your credit card pay

As well as saving you money on cheque costs and giving you extra offset on your redraw account, paying by credit card can actually save you cash.

Most cards offer reward points that can be exchanged for a voucher at a department store or similar. Use the money to buy something you were going to buy anyway, even if it is just a present for someone.

If you use your card to pay large fixed expenses such as council rates, car, house and health insurance payments, you can build up points quite quickly. Add major appliances, petrol, presents and clothes and your points could be worth $100 or more within a year.

Don't forget you must have the type of card that gives you up to 55 days free credit and you must pay the whole balance when you get the statement so you don't pay interest.

Reduce vehicle costs

There are a lot of expenses in owning a vehicle, and there may be scope for saving here. There is:

- the initial cost of the vehicle;
- interest costs if you buy your car on credit;
- registration;
- insurance;
- repairs and servicing;
- tyres and batteries; and
- petrol.

Pay cash for your car

Paying cash for your car will save the interest costs entirely and your insurance will cost less.

Buy a second-hand car

Cars lose more of their value in the first two years than they do in the following years. You can buy a two to three-year-old Falcon or Commodore for not much more than half the cost of a new car. Small cars and four-wheel-drives tend to keep their value a little better than this. It is not long before your brand new car is no longer brand new. Let someone else pay for the luxury of owning a brand new car, and buy yours near new or second-hand.

Many companies and fleet providers sell their cars when they have done 40 000 kilometres, so there is usually a good supply of two to three year-old cars available.

Buy a smaller car

You will save on every single one of these vehicle costs if you buy a smaller car. Have the smallest car that you can manage with. Almost any car these days can pull a trailer.

Small cars use less fuel than large cars. A large four-wheel-drive can easily use three times as much fuel as a small car.

If you do 20 000 kilometres in a year, this could cost you over $2000 a year more in fuel.

A smaller car uses cheaper tyres, and may be cheaper to register and cheaper to insure.

Hatchbacks, vans and small four-wheel-drives will fit more luggage, shopping and sports gear than a sedan.

One car or two

Some families need two cars, some families don't. If the main income earner has a company car or can easily commute to work, then you only need one car in your family. This is a huge saving over owning two cars.

However, if the main income earner needs a vehicle for work, and the other partner and the children are left relying on buses for shopping, getting to school and after-school recreation, then only owning one car may reduce your lifestyle more than the extra saving is worth. Don't deprive your children of the transport they need to attend after-school activities, other children's parties, or force them to walk long distances to school in wet weather just to save the cost of a car you could easily afford.

Reduce petrol costs

You can reduce petrol costs by:

- filling your tank when petrol is discounted, even if it is still half full;
- combining trips, for example, shop when you pick up the children from school;
- shopping locally when you can;
- shopping efficiently, so you buy most of your week's groceries in one trip; and

- driving more slowly—you will use less petrol (and avoid speeding fines).

Look after your car

If you keep your car regularly serviced it will last longer. If you keep the interior clean and the exterior polished it will be worth more when you come to replace it.

Don't move house too often

When you move house you pay stamp duty, bank fees if you have a mortgage, estate agent's commission, solicitor's or settlement agent's fees, and removal expenses.

Before you sell up and move, think about the alternatives. If you are transferred in your job, you may be better off in the long term by renting out your home, and renting a home in the new location. The catch appears to be the fact that you pay tax on the rent you receive, but you can't claim a deduction for the house that you rent. Remember though, you can claim for other costs relating to your home, like rates and repairs while it is rented out, and the interest you are paying on your mortgage. Overall you are likely to better off than paying the costs of buying and selling.

If you need a larger home, think about extensions or a second storey before you put your house on the market.

Most people can't afford to buy their dream home first up. You may need a larger home as your children grow up, and when your children move out you may want a smaller home. That's three homes altogether. Choose carefully where you would like to live and think about the possibility of future extensions when you buy a home.

You can improve your financial situation, however, by buying a run-down home in a good area, doing it up and selling it at a profit. You then buy another run-down home and repeat the process. After a while you will not need a mortgage at all. But if you do this, keep the hidden costs in mind and make sure you really are making a profit.

Do it yourself

It is cheaper to do a lot of things yourself rather than paying someone else to do them. This depends on your skills, on the amount of spare time you have and whether you can use your spare time on money-making activities. For most people it is cheaper to:

- do your own ironing and housework;
- wash your own windows;
- wash and polish your own car;
- bath your dog yourself;
- mow your own lawns;
- weed your own garden;
- steam clean your carpets yourself;
- mend or service your own car (if you know how);
- change your watch battery yourself;
- grow your own plants;
- grow your own fruit and vegetables;
- lay paving yourself;
- paint your house yourself;
- build your pergola yourself;
- put in reticulation yourself; and
- cut your children's hair.

Making your own clothes and soft furnishings is generally cheaper, but you need the skill and enthusiasm, and you need to actually complete the job. Half finished projects are no use to anyone.

There are some jobs, such as plumbing and electrical work, that you are not allowed to do yourself, and some jobs, such as cutting down trees, where it is safer to bring in an expert. You don't save at all doing some things yourself, like delivering letters for example.

Avoid money-wasting habits

There are ways to arrange your shopping and your lifestyle so you don't waste money on buying things you don't need.

Take a list with you when you shop. Not just for groceries, for everything. If you see something you just have to have that is not on your list, go home and think about it. You may decide you don't really want it.

Don't shop when you are hungry. You will reach the checkout with a trolley load of junk food. Take a snack and a drink with you if you are out for a whole morning or are shopping on your way home from work.

Shop without your children. I don't think I need to elaborate too much on this. Children can spend money much faster than adults can earn it.

Don't shop just for entertainment. If you have an hour or two to fill, go to a library, not a shopping centre.

Avoid panic buying by planning ahead. If you realise the day before a wedding or other major event that your best dress has mysteriously become much too tight since you last wore it, or your only suit is ten years out of date and full of moth holes, you will spend more money replacing these items in a hurry than you would if you had three or four weeks to shop around.

Make lists for parties, Christmas and other celebrations ahead of time, so you are not making last minute trips to town for something you have forgotten.

Stay away from bargain stores. Bargain stores are full of useless things that are attractive and low priced. Keep children out of bargain stores.

Don't read mail order catalogues when you have nothing else to do. The mail order people are marvellous at inventing things that people have no earthly use for but must have.

Don't go into clothing stores every time you go shopping just to see what's new. Only go into clothing stores if clothes are on your shopping list.

Don't allow yourself to indulge in compulsive buying habits. If every time you go to the supermarket you come back with a new kitchen gadget, a pair of socks or a new lipstick, you have a habit that is costing you money you could be putting towards your mortgage.

Don't buy things you won't use

Most of us have spent money at some time on things that we didn't wear or use. Most of us have at least one pair of jeans or shoes that fitted in the shop but were too small when we got them home. Clothes may shrink in the wash, but they don't shrink in transport!

This is wasted money. While the odd unnecessary purchase is probably inevitable, we can reduce this type of mistake by shopping more carefully.

This applies to:

- clothes you end up never wearing;
- fabric and wool that sits hoarded in a cupboard and is never made into anything useful;
- make-up that you never get around to using;
- power tools that are used once or not at all;
- kitchen gadgets that are used once or not at all;
- ornaments that don't actually do a job;
- collectables; and
- books you never read.

Try to weed these things out of your shopping before you reach the checkout. You can't eliminate mistakes entirely, but you can reduce them by thinking about the things you buy more carefully. Do you need the item? If not, why are you buying it?

If you are a home sewer or knitter, don't hoard fabric or wool. Finish one garment before you buy the fabric or wool for the next one.

Some homes have collections of expensive power tools languishing in the shed, waiting for the project that you never get around to starting. Most homes have heaps of weird kitchen appliances that do nothing but waste cupboard space.

There are some kitchen appliances that really do make the job easier. Popcorn makers, breadmakers, mixers, slicers and electric toasters all do the job better than you can without them. Some kitchen gadgets are more useful than others, and some are more useful to some people than others. A mixer is fine if you use it, but it becomes a useless heap of plastic and metal if you never make cakes. Are you really going to make pies if you buy that piemaker, when you have never made them with a pie dish and an oven available? And have you made waffles with the waffle-making gismo more than once in the five years since you bought it?

Ask yourself whenever you are thinking about buying something whether you will really use it, or whether you are only buying it because it looks like a bargain, is pretty, looks as though it might be useful sometime, or comes with a free gift or a chance to win a holiday.

You only need one toaster, electric kettle, mixer, calculator, kitchen timer, iron, hair dryer, watch, umbrella, alarm clock, electric drill, vacuum cleaner and computer. If you replace an appliance, throw the old one out. If you are not prepared to throw the old one out, you don't need the new one.

If you buy something that doesn't do what it is supposed to, take it back and get a refund. Always keep receipts and guarantees for appliances.

Avoid bringing junk home

Junk is anything you own that you don't eat, wear, use, read or enjoy owning. Most of us have heaps of junk that we have become so attached to we would never even think of getting rid of it.

As well as the initial cost, junk costs money to store, maintain and insure. Avoiding junk is a whole new way of looking at the things you own. Ultimately you may decide you need to move to a larger house, just because you have too much junk to fit in your current home.

If you avoid spending money on things you are unlikely to use, you are part of the way to avoiding junk. The rest of the way is to stop hoarding things that have no immediate use, and not much prospect of future use.

Junk costs money

Here is an example of junk costing you money. Imagine you run out of cupboard space and buy a new cupboard for $200 that would fit nicely into a spare corner of your laundry. Let's have a look at what is in the old cupboard that was full. Here are some of the things we might find:

- Three boxes of supermarket plastic bags. We use those as bin liners, but do we really need three boxes of them?
- Some worn-out towels. We use those sometimes to mop up spills, but do we ever use all fifteen of them?
- Old t-shirts. We use those to polish the car. We have twenty t-shirts and the car is only polished twice a year.
- A box of empty jam jars. One day we may grow enough fruit to make jam.
- A broken suitcase. It only needs the catch replaced.
- An old record player and records. We have CDs now.
- Leftover fabric scraps. Well, we just might get around to making a patchwork quilt out of them.

We just spent $200 on a cupboard. If we had thrown all this lot out, we wouldn't have needed the new cupboard at all. Junk costs money.

Before you run out and buy a new cupboard or bookcase or build a new shed because you have run out of space, or even move to a larger house, ask yourself a few questions.

Are your cupboards full of supermarket bags, obsolete towels, empty jars or hoarded baby clothes? Are your sheds full of rusting cans of paint, offcuts of wood from long past projects, power tools that no longer work, broken television sets, old parts from cars you no longer own and bicycles that nobody rides?

Clear out your junk

Have a cleanout of all your cupboards and all your sheds. Throw out the rubbish. Put anything you don't want that is saleable to one side. Give anything useful but not saleable that you no longer want to charity. Then tidy the things you do want back into the cupboard or shed. You will have heaps more room and may save on buying extra storage.

Now have a garage sale or take your unwanted things to a swap meet. Large items can be advertised for sale on local boards and in local newspapers. Put the proceeds from selling your junk towards your home loan.

You may be more willing to part with things if you can get a few dollars for them than if you give them away. Children are more ready to part with outgrown toys if they can sell them for even a small amount of money.

Don't buy jewellery or ornaments

Reduce what you spend on jewellery, ornaments, artwork, collections and craft. Jewellery loses value the moment you take it out of the shop. You need to store it in a safe and insure it, so there are ongoing costs. If you buy presents of jewellery for your partner, buy chocolates or flowers instead and put the rest of the money towards your mortgage.

Ornaments may enhance your life, but usually they just sit and get dusty, and after the first rapture of owning them, you scarcely see them at all. You need to buy shelves and cupboards to display them and again, you pay to insure them. Keep ornaments to a minimum.

While it is great to have a few pictures on the walls, they don't need to be expensive originals. Buy second-hand pictures at swap meets, or posters. They will cost less and you can afford to change them occasionally. If your children are good at art, hang their work up. Children usually paint lovely bright pictures at school and they will mean more to you than conventional artwork.

Collections can take a lot of time, money, storage space, security and insurance (again!). Ask yourself whether that collection is really worth the cost. If it is, fine, but do think about it, and don't just collect things for fashion or for the sake of it. If your collection is for investment, think about whether the money that you spend on it could work harder in more conventional investments.

Craft of all types can be a wonderfully relaxing hobby, but it can also be expensive. If you like craftwork, at least try to finish each piece before you start the next, and try to choose less expensive craft types. If you can use the product, either for yourself or as a gift, all the better.

A lot of craft these days is expensive and high fashion. There are lots of traditional crafts that are more skillful and more rewarding, and there are community craft groups and cheap community-based courses for all kinds of hobbies. Libraries have books on most kinds of craft.

Have a cheaper Christmas

If your family celebrates Christmas, there are subtle ways of making this work for you. Look at all the costs of Christmas and decide where you can save without making any difference to the pleasure. The joy of Christmas is usually getting the family together at the same time in a party atmosphere. The cost of the presents, the food or the decorations has no bearing on the enjoyment.

Parties

If all your relatives converge on your house for Christmas dinner every year, suggest you go to someone else's next year. If this doesn't work, suggest they bring something to contribute to the meal or the drinks. You can do this in a polite way.

It is nice to have a few special foods at Christmas, but keep things rational. Buying wine that is a dollar or two a bottle cheaper will save you a lot and only wine buffs will notice. Wine buffs will probably bring their own wine anyway.

An un-iced Christmas cake, a packet of roll-out icing, a few drops of food colour, some small Christmas cutters and a bit of plastic holly cost dollars less than an iced cake. All you need then is one or two enthusiastic small children to make your un-iced cake into an iced and decorated masterpiece.

Presents outwards

Suggest that your relatives only buy presents for children and not adults. Or alternatively that only small presents are bought for the adults. That should save quite a lot. You can buy yourself something you actually want with the money you save. If your relatives throw up their hands in horror at this suggestion, buy them the small presents anyway. Next year they will do the same.

Look for bargains that will make good presents throughout the year, starting with the after-Christmas sales. You will need to keep track of what you have bought for whom but a list will make this easy. Be careful with use by dates. Giving chocolates that expired the previous April rather gives the game away.

Presents inwards

If you get lots of presents from relatives that you send straight to a charity store, you are missing out on a chance to save money. Ask your relatives for things you actually need, or will at least use. Give them a list, and be prepared to be a bit flexible. If you ask for socks and they turn up bright orange with purple teddy bears, at least you can hide them under boots and save wear on socks you do like.

Lists may not seem as romantic, but then there is nothing romantic about getting a gift that you don't want. Most people's relatives will welcome a list, because it makes their Christmas shopping less of a headache. In this age of everyone having everything, present shopping can become a chore. Most adults have no idea what to buy other people's children, so lists from children will probably be appreciated, but make sure the list does not contain hard-to-get or expensive items.

Stay out of debt

If you have a credit card choose the type with 55 days interest free, keep careful track of everything you put on the card and pay off the whole amount by the date due, every time.

Credit cards are really useful things if you use them properly. A credit card can:

- save you money on bank transaction fees and debits tax;
- allow you to earn interest or offset for longer on the money in your bank account; and
- gain reward points that you can redeem for something you would have bought anyway.

But credit cards can be a trap. Every year thousands of ordinary Australians run up credit card debts that they can't pay back. Some people go bankrupt because they can't handle credit. And credit costs money. You pay around 15 per cent interest on credit cards, 20 per cent if they are issued by a department store.

If you always pay the whole balance on your card and never pay interest, great. If you don't pay the full amount and do pay interest, you need to change your ways starting from today.

Credit is not just negative savings; it's expensive negative savings. If you have a credit card debt that is too high to pay off on your next statement, you need to do two things. You need to stop buying things that you can't afford, and you need to clear the credit card debt before you start to fast-track your mortgage. It is a bit pointless putting in extra money to pay off a loan at 7 per cent, when you are borrowing money at around 15 per cent on your credit card.

If you know you are a credit card addict, then cut the cards up, or run a large magnet over them so they don't work any more. But keep in mind that if you can use your card properly, it can work for you and save you money.

Staying out of debt doesn't stop at credit cards. Obviously there is nothing wrong with having a mortgage, but there are other sorts of consumer loans that you can avoid with better money management.

If you are starting out in your first job and you need your own transport, you may need to borrow money to buy a car. This should be the only time you ever borrow money for a private vehicle.

Never borrow money for holidays. Borrowing for holidays is *have-now-pay-later* at its very worst. When you return from the holiday you have a huge debt to pay, and only a few photos to show for it. Save up for holidays, you will appreciate them more.

Change your attitude to money

Before you go out and start saving money in any of these ways, change the way you think about money.

In addition to ideas I've mentioned earlier, there are three other things you can think about when you shop that may make you think twice about wasting money on things you don't need:

1. how long it took you to earn the money;
2. what else you could do with the money; and
3. are you being persuaded to buy something you don't need?

Money and time

Money is finite in a similar way to time, because money and time are directly related. All your money has been obtained by someone giving up his or her time to earn it. It may have been you, your partner, or a relative who left you the money. But it was still someone's time, a portion of someone's lifetime. You only get investment income because you had money to invest that you or someone else earned. If you are on social security, someone earned that money and paid it as tax before it came to you. Even if your money came from winning Lotto, the money you won was earned by other Lotto players who bought tickets in the draw.

Money involves opportunity cost

Money is finite. The things available for you to spend it on are more or less infinite. However much you have, you could spend more. When you spend money you are making a choice to buy one thing and not another, and to spend rather than to save. Make the choice to spend consciously, knowing that you are doing without something else, that you are reducing your available funds.

Keep at least some sort of global perspective when you spend money. We are better off than most of the world's people and we tend to see the value of money only in the context of our own society. We pay $30 for a haircut or a restaurant meal without thinking twice about it. If we give $30 to a third world charity we think of ourselves as being generous. Yet the $30 will go a lot further than a haircut or a single meal in a third world country. It could improve the lives of people who live on subsistence incomes and don't always have even the basic needs of life. It could make life a lot easier for someone, somewhere.

I am not suggesting that you don't have haircuts or eat out, only that you think of the value of the money when you spend it and the opportunity cost of your spending choices.

Money and consumers

The aim of the companies that sell us goods and services is to make profits. And a lot of those goods are perfectly useless, or are much more expensive than they need to be because you are paying extra for a brand name, a picture of a film or television character or for a slogan. Brand names and royalties on film characters and slogans are all that some companies actually own. They merely arrange production, distribution and marketing of their branded products without owning the factories that produce the goods, the trucks that transport them or the warehouses and shops that sell them.

Companies move production to third world countries and justify it because it makes the world more efficient. Labour is cheap in some places in the world. Goods are made in those places. Consumer cash (and consumer credit) are available in other places in the world. The goods are sold there. We get lots of efficiently produced goods and catch phrases like 'increased productivity' and 'global economy'. They are euphemisms for increasing company profits by exploiting low-cost labour.

Consumer spending is good for the economy. If we don't spend, fewer people are employed, more welfare is paid, and higher taxes are needed. Our standard of living will be lower. If everyone in Australia decided to stop spending money they don't actually have on things they don't need we might be in trouble. Certainly we would need to start looking at managing our economy in a different way, and this might well be a better way. But think about this. Do the rich spend all their money? They may spend a lot, but if they spent it all they wouldn't be rich. The economy will not collapse because you as an individual or family decide not to spend everything you earn and more besides.

A lot of the things that we spend money on are really of no earthly use to anybody. Things we do need have come down in price so everyone (or at least everyone with a job) can afford them. So now the entrepreneurs want us to buy heaps of things we don't need so the profits keep coming in. Manufacturers keep inventing more and more things because entrepreneurs know that consumers will keep buying until they run out of money, get into debt and then still spend more. The rich make profits and the poor are kept that way.

Don't waste your money on junk

Look in any discount gift store. There are lots of totally useless things that people buy just because they are cheap and attractive.

And these gismos are self-proliferating. Instead of one action character toy, there are 150 to collect, and a book listing them so you know you haven't missed any out. Instead of one teddy, you buy 50 different coloured ones. Collect them all. And when you have collected them all, new ones will be released.

Fashion clothing is another area where we tend to spend much more than we need. We throw out our jeans with zippers because this year we are supposed to wear jeans with buttons. Maybe next year jeans with zippers will be back but we can't use our old ones because the new ones will be flares.

We are being exploited as consumers by the people who make profits from persuading us to buy things we don't need.

Think before you buy

Before you buy anything like this that you don't really need, stop and think about where your money is going. Think about the underpaid workers who are totally unable to afford to buy the things they produce, about the rich raking in the profits and the brand name royalties, and about the widening national and global rich–poor divide. By buying all these useless products, we are contributing to a world where a minority of the world's people owns a majority of the world's wealth.

I am not saying there is anything wrong with capitalism, although the current economic rationalist breed of capitalism has its faults. Capitalism in the abstract appears to be the best system we have devised so far to organise society and improve living standards. Efficiency, productivity and sound economic management probably are the way forward to improving the lot of humankind, however slow the process may be. Communism did not, in the end, work. And the division of society into rich and poor has been with us since we first tilled the land and invented settlements and civilisation.

What I am offering you is a way of looking at money that will help you to think about what you are buying and why you are buying it. Everytime you take out your purse or wallet think it through.

- Do I need this?
- Will I really use or wear it?
- Can I buy this cheaper elsewhere?
- Where will I put it when I get it home?
- How long did it take to earn the money?
- What else could I do with the money?
- Am I being exploited as a consumer?

I am not suggesting that you do without things that you need and things that make life easier and more pleasant. I am suggesting that you don't just spend money for the sake of it on mindless junk that is put in front of you in shops or advertised on television.

How long did it take you or your partner to earn the money for that $12 mug featuring a joke about an overweight cartoon cat? You can buy a plain mug in a supermarket for only $2. The extra $10 could feed a child in Africa for a month. Do you need that fancy moving lamp that won't provide enough light for anything, or will you pay the $100 off your mortgage? Will the fish plaque that sings when someone walks past drive you crazy in a month's time? Do your children really need to collect the whole 100 soft beanie toys, or will one or two favourites be sufficient? Is it worth paying $30 for a t-shirt just because it has a picture of a pop star or a top clothing brand name on the front?

If you like to wear t-shirts with slogans on, buy a plain

Australian made t-shirt for $10 from a discount department store, find an indelible felt-tip pen and write on the front of it:

Capitalism is a Con

Will you be a good little exploited sheep and buy all this silly stuff that is put in front of you by rich entrepreneurs to tempt you to part with your money? Or will you use your money to pay off your mortgage and then invest in the companies that make all the profits?

Life after mortgage 6

So, you have finally paid off your mortgage, the bank has given you back the title deed to your home and you now have an extra $1000 a month to spend on clothes, CDs, eating out, holidays and the like. Right?

No way! You may have paid off your mortgage, but you are still only halfway there. You are now going to use what you save to fund your retirement. You now have an extra $1000 or so a month to set up a retirement plan so you can retire wealthy and never have to bother about assets tests, deeming rates or Centrelink queues. (Substitute your own loan payoff amount for the $1000 in this section.)

You may decide at this point that you need a bigger house. You have a lot of equity in your home now, and you can move if you want to, and start paying off another mortgage. While you are choosing a new home and preparing to move, put the money into a bank account or term deposit.

Invest your repayment money

Don't spend the money on something else for even one month. Have a celebration by all means, but the first month you no longer have a mortgage to pay, put the money into some sort of investment, or store it in a bank account for investing later.

You may need to save the first two or three months' payments before you invest the money, as there are overheads involved, and many funds will not take small investment amounts. If you don't trust any investments except money in the bank, then put your money into term deposits or bank bonds and you will still retire wealthy. But still read through this section. You may be surprised how easy it is to invest safely in investments with a higher or more tax effective return.

Table 6.1 shows how $1000 invested per month can grow into a huge retirement benefit over several years. If you have paid off your loan over 15 years, you may have another 25 years to save before you retire. There is also a very large table of investment returns at the back of this book and instructions on how to use it.

Yes, the last figure on this table really is over $23 million. You are unlikely to sustain 20 per cent return on your savings after tax over this length of time, but some managed funds have earned well over 15 per cent for the last five years. Your

Table 6.1 Investment returns for $1000 per month

Yrs	per mth	5%	7%	10%	12%	15%	20%
5	1000	68 289	72 011	78 082	82 486	89 682	103 454
10	1000	155 929	174 094	206 552	232 339	278 657	382 364
15	1000	268 403	318 811	417 924	504 576	676 863	1 134 295
20	1000	412 746	523 965	765 697	999 148	1 515 955	3 161 479
25	1000	597 991	814 797	1 337 890	1 897 635	3 284 074	8 626 708
30	1000	835 726	1 227 087	2 279 325	3 529 914	7 009 821	23 360 802

money will not be worth as much in 30 years' time because of inflation, but it will be worth a lot more than the nothing you will have if you don't save at all. You can increase the amount you contribute over the years as your salary increases and this will help to counteract the inflation effect.

Choosing investments

Choosing where to invest your money can be a little daunting if you have been concentrating on paying off your mortgage and you don't know much about investing. When you are close to paying off your mortgage, start reading investment books and magazines, so you are familiar with the options available to you. The more you know about investing money, the more likely you are to get it right. However, there are lazy ways to invest effectively, and we will cover these further on.

Most people are quite capable of investing themselves. To invest yourself you need to:

- take the trouble to find out the options available;
- diversify your investments; and
- avoid being tempted to gamble in risky investments for high promised returns.

You may want the advice of a financial planner, but they do tend to recommend the investments that give them the maximum amount of commission. Occasionally the odd one is dishonest and unfortunate retirees lose spectacular sums in failed investments. The more you know about investment, the less likely you are to be persuaded into things that benefit the financial planner more than they benefit you. However, if you don't have the time or expertise to invest yourself, there are

Spreadsheet tip

If you want to set the investment return table on an Excel spreadsheet, the function you need is called Future Value. The formula for future value is:

= FV(rate per period, no. of periods, – payment per period, – starting value, type).

You will need to divide the annual rate by 12 as you are working in months. The starting value is zero, as we are starting with nothing and the type is 1, because we are adding our payment at the beginning of the month.

Future value is not easy to work out on a standard calculator. Some scientific calculators have it as an available function. For anyone who is interested in how it is done, the formula for the future value of an investment is

$$\text{Future Value} = P \times (1 + r)^n$$

P is the amount invested
r is the interest rate per period
n is the number of periods

This, however, only gives you a value for the first amount you invest. Here we are putting in another $1000 each month. The future value of the following month's payment would be the same calculation for one less month. You could in theory calculate this for each monthly investment, then add them together. However, if you are not using a spreadsheet, it is easier to use the tables at the back of this book.

plenty of excellent financial planners and investment products available. If you deal with a reputable firm you can be confident of receiving quality service.

Investment categories

There are three places you can invest your money:

1. fixed interest securities;
2. property; and
3. shares.

There is also a fourth category that includes works of art, wine, antiques, classic cars and gold, but these are specialist investments and I am not covering them here.

With a fixed interest security, such as a term deposit or a bank bond, you are lending your money to the institution for a set interest rate. You are paid the interest, and your capital is returned intact at the end of the term. You pay tax on the interest, but get no allowance for inflation. Your capital is actually worth less at the end than it was in the beginning. The advantage of fixed interest securities is that you are unlikely to lose your capital. The disadvantage is that you don't get as high a return as you might on property and shares.

With property, you are buying a fixed asset that may give you a rental return, and should appreciate in value at least at the inflation rate. The return will go up each year as rents increase with inflation. Your capital is growing, and your return is also growing. If you sell the asset, the capital gain is taxed at a concessional rate. The advantage of property is that it is unlikely to decrease much in price, and historically the returns are quite high. The disadvantage of owning property directly is the illiquid nature of the investment. If you need the money for something else it may take months to sell the property, and the selling costs are high.

When you buy shares, you become a part owner of a company that is using its assets to make profits. The value of the company will go up as the assets of the company increase, and your dividend will go up if the company profits go up each year. Your capital is growing with the increasing value of the assets of the company and your dividend is (hopefully) increasing each year. As with property, the capital appreciation is taxed at a concessional rate. The advantages of shares are that they tend to offer the best return on your money, and you can sell your shares at any time for a small cost. However, share prices can be quite volatile, so you have no guarantee that the value of your asset will increase with time, and companies can occasionally fail completely, taking all of your money with them.

Both property and shares protect the value of your capital from inflation. Fixed interest investments don't.

Direct and indirect investment

You can invest in all three categories directly, by buying a bank bond, buying a house or commercial unit, or buying shares in a company. Or you can invest in a managed fund that pools the savings of a lot of investors so the fund can invest in a larger range of investments than a single investor could afford to buy. There are managed funds for all three investment categories and funds which invest in a mix of all three. Managed funds are also called investment trusts and unit trusts. I have used these terms interchangeably.

It is best to have a mix of property, shares and fixed interest investments. Some people like property and distrust shares.

Some people love the sharemarket and think property is for old-fashioned investors. Some people won't invest their money outside of a bank. If any of these categories sounds like you, try investing about 30 per cent of your savings in managed funds in the categories you don't like as much. You will be less subject to boom and bust in a particular category. There are times when interest rates are low on fixed interest securities. There are times when property is oversupplied and commercial units languish untenanted or drop in value. There are sharemarket crashes, where the value of your investments can drop dramatically overnight. These setbacks rarely occur all at once.

If you distrust investments and want to leave your money in the bank, then do so. You will still retire wealthy if you earn a reasonable rate on your savings. Avoid savings accounts paying low rates of interest. Term deposits are usually a reliable way of obtaining a reasonable return for little investment effort.

Diversify

The single most important rule when you invest is to diversify your investments. If you are investing in anything but cash in the bank, don't put all of your money into one investment scheme, or even one investment type. There is luck as well as skill in investment. Hedge your bets.

This is the single most important rule for investing, yet many people just simply ignore it and invest all their funds in risky schemes with high promised returns. Diversify your investments.

If you are investing in shares, property trusts or managed funds, try to have a maximum of 5 per cent to 10 per cent of your money in any one investment. Spread your investments over different categories and different fund managers.

Obviously the day you transfer your first $2000 to an investment, you will have all of your money in one investment. Choose something safe to start with, such as an investment fund run by a bank. Continue to invest in lots of around $2000 in different investments until you have around 20 investments, spread over a range of types and industries. Start with really safe things like balanced funds and cash management trusts, then add property trusts, and listed or unlisted share trusts. After this add blue-chip shares, then smaller companies, and finally more speculative shares if this interests you.

When you have built up a range of investments, you can increase the amount you put into each investment, or add to existing investments. If you continue to put $2000 into new investments, you could eventually find yourself with shares in two or three hundred different companies. Keeping track of this might be a pleasant hobby for your retirement years, but it could become a nightmare when you come to fill in your tax return each year.

Increase the size of each investment as your wealth increases, and add to your previous investments if you are happy with the way they are performing. It is usually fairly easy to add more money to a managed fund and you can buy more shares in a company you already own shares in. Twenty to 30 investments are all most people would want to keep track of, but this is up to you. Aim for at least ten, so if one fails it will not be a major disaster for you.

Over the years there have been many cases of investments failing totally. It doesn't happen often, but it does happen. Some of these investments would have seemed as safe as houses to perfectly intelligent investors. Several property trusts failed in the 1980s, and more recently we have had a mortgage broking scandal in Western Australia and the collapse of a large Australian insurance company.

Some of these collapses took with them the entire savings of dozens of retirees, who could never, ever hope to save that kind of money again. I know there are more important things in life than money, but it would have been devastating for these people to lose everything they had saved over the years for their retirement. Worry about money does not help anybody to live a long and happy life, especially if you are no longer working or able to work.

This shouldn't happen to you if you avoid putting all of your money into one scheme, however safe and attractive that investment may seem.

Never get talked into in any investment scheme that you don't understand or are not entirely happy about. And don't throw diversification out the window for the promise of high returns or large tax deductions.

Risk and return

If you take higher risks in investing you may get a higher return, but you may also lose your money. In general, the safer the investment, the lower the return will be, with money in the bank the safest option. If you want to try a few really high-risk things, such as shares in gold explorers or biotechnology companies, investment funds that deal in options and futures (hedge funds), or funds that invest in small companies, this is fine. Money should always be fun. But don't risk more than 10 per cent of your money in speculative schemes. If you make a profit, take it out and put it into something safer, and just retain the 10 per cent in the speculative ventures. If you make losses, don't keep putting more money in to try to get back what you lost.

If you find you love speculating, and you're good at speculating (there is definitely luck as well as skill here), and you have saved enough in safe investments to live on forever, then increase this proportion if you want to. However, never lose sight of your aim of retiring with money working for you.

Fixed interest investments

If you like to keep some or all of your money in the bank, you can leave it in a savings account, a term deposit, or put it into bank investment bonds. For short-term parking of large sums of money, there are cash management accounts, cash management trusts and bank bills. All these investments are totally safe. Your interest will be paid at the agreed rate, and your capital will be returned intact at the end of the term.

Some managed trusts and investment books will distinguish between cash and fixed interest. Cash is money invested for less than one year, in cash management accounts, bank bills or other short-term investments. Fixed interest usually refers to investments with a term greater than one year, such as bonds.

Savings accounts

Most banks only offer a lousy 1.5 per cent–2 per cent on savings accounts, but there are some better options if you are prepared to shop around. Most banks offer a bonus savings account where you gain extra interest during months where you deposit money and don't withdraw any. If you buy and sell shares through a broker, you can usually have a cash management account with a reasonable interest rate.

At the time of writing several major financial institutions are offering a high interest savings account that you link to your normal account at your usual bank. You transfer funds in when you like, and can withdraw on a day's notice. This savings account cannot have a cheque facility or a keycard, but the interest rate is very competitive. This may be a catalyst for other banks to offer better savings products to their customers.

Term deposits

Term deposits usually pay a higher interest rate than a savings account, provided the term is long enough and the amount is high enough. They are useful for parking large sums of money that you don't need at present, and are the best bank investment product for most people.

Banks will often have a special term with a slightly higher interest rate. Take this term, and when the deposit matures, take the term with the best interest rate again.

Bank investment bonds

Investment bonds work like a term deposit with a term from three to ten years, and a better interest rate. There is normally a minimum of $5000 that can be invested, and only some banks offer them. These are excellent for people who like to keep their money safely in the bank, because the interest rate is higher than for term deposits.

Other bonds and debentures

There are lots of other sorts of government and semi-government bonds. Debentures are a similar fixed interest product offered by large companies. Bonds and debentures are sometimes advertised in newspapers. Your bank, stockbroker or financial adviser can give you details of any currently available.

Cash management accounts

Cash management accounts are normally at call accounts, so your money is available whenever you want it. The interest rates are usually better than a normal savings account, but less than a term deposit. The interest varies according to the balance in your account, but is usually still quite low unless you have more than $50 000. However, some banks currently give you a reasonably good rate from around $5000, so ask around. If you go below the minimum, you can still keep the account open, but you get no interest at all.

Cash management trusts

A cash management trust is an investment fund that deals in fixed interest and cash securities. They usually give a good rate for small amounts, but there may be a minimum investment amount of $2000 or even $5000. Most banks and companies that deal in managed investments run these. There may be entry fees, so look out for this.

Bank bills

Bank bills are good for large amounts of money for short lengths of time, but they are normally for amounts of $50 000 or more and hence outside the scope of most ordinary investors. However, one major bank now offers bank bills for amounts as low as $10 000, and these can even be bought or sold on the Internet.

Bank bills come in anything from 30 days to six months. You buy the bill for less than its face value, and the bank gives you the face value at the maturity date of the bill. Your interest is the difference between what you pay for the bill and its value at maturity. For a bill for $100 000 paying 5 per cent for 30 days, you would pay around $99 590 for the bill and collect $100 000 after 30 days. The interest rate is usually better than for a term deposit, but you will pay a brokerage fee.

Remember to take the brokerage into consideration when comparing the rate on bank bills with other types of investment. A brokerage charge of 0.3 per cent may not sound much, but if you buy a 180-day bank bill it will reduce the interest rate by 0.6 per cent per annum and for a 90-day bank bill by 1.2 per cent.

Listed income securities

This is a relatively new type of investment that started from late 1999, caught on quickly, then went a little out of favour. Income securities are normally issued by a major company, such as National Australia Bank or Woolworths, and work like a loan to the company. You can subscribe when these are first released at an issue price, usually $100 per security, or you can buy them later on the stock exchange through a broker. The company will not, however, buy the security back from you. If you want to redeem your securities, you will have to sell them to someone else.

The interest rate is normally floating, and is 1 per cent to 2 per cent higher than the current market rate, so if interest rates go up or down, the income security rate follows. This will normally give you a rate higher than a term deposit. The interest is normally paid twice a year to holders of the notes at a certain date, so keep this in mind when you buy and sell your notes.

Income securities tend to trade at around their issue price or slightly lower, so you can buy in when you like and sell when you like, but you will pay brokerage when you buy or sell. To gain with these, you need a time horizon of a year or more, to allow for the cost of the brokerage and still be better off than a term deposit.

Property

Most people are happy having money in property. Property does appreciate considerably over the long term, but it is often in short bursts, with a long period in between where prices stay relatively stable.

Property is always considered a safe investment. There may be the odd time when property drops in value, but this is mainly after a huge and unsustainable rise in prices. If you retired with three or four rental houses which were fully paid off, you would have a reasonable retirement income which was fairly reliable, and went up with inflation as rents rose. Remembering that you get rental income to help pay off the mortgage, this would be quite achievable for most families over their working life.

Improving your home

For most people, buying their own home is the first place they invest their money. If you have a mortgage, paying off your mortgage faster is usually the best way to invest your money because the after-tax return is equal to your home loan rate.

You can also put your savings into improving your home, but beware of over-capitalisation. If you live in a street of ordinary houses worth around $150 000 (for example), spending $50 000 on improving your home will not necessarily mean that you get $50 000 more for it if you sell it. People with $200 000 to spend on a home may not want to live in a street of $150 000 homes, however nice you have made the house with the additions.

When you have paid off your mortgage (or any time before or after this) you can upgrade to a larger house or a house in a better neighbourhood, and start paying off a new mortgage. You may want to carry on doing this until you retire.

However, suppose you were by then living in a home worth $600 000, but you had only $100 000 saved in other investments. You would have to sell your home and buy a cheaper one to release the money to give you enough income to retire on. You may think now that you would be prepared to do this, but will you still think that at the time? It is very hard to move to a less desirable area, and even harder to move to a smaller house. You also may not want to move away from your current friends and neighbours.

Savings invested in your own home will grow at the rate that property appreciates, but this may not be as much as you would have got for that money invested elsewhere. But there is no tax to pay on the capital appreciation during the time you own your home, and you will not pay any CGT when you sell. And let's face it, you have to live somewhere so it may as well be somewhere pleasant. Just make sure you also invest enough elsewhere so you are not forced to sell your home to release your retirement savings.

If you enjoy improving homes, painting, adding pergolas, laying paving, gardening and so forth, you can increase your wealth substantially by buying a run-down home in a good area, living in it for a year or two while you make the house more attractive, selling at a profit (no CGT on your own home, remember), and buying another run-down home in a good area.

Holiday homes

You can use your retirement plan savings to buy a holiday home. Again, you will not get the return on it that you might elsewhere (unless you rent it out to other people for their holidays).

Remember that if you buy a holiday home that you do not rent out, you are tying up capital that could be earning an income, as well as gaining in capital value. Imagine you bought a holiday home for $150 000. If you had put that money into a rental property, you would get an annual income of around $6000 before tax, and at least $3000 after tax. If you had put it into a listed share trust, paying 5 per cent dividend fully franked, you would have between $5500 and $7500 depending on your tax rate. (We will look at listed share trusts in the sharemarket section.) In both instances you would get a similar capital appreciation as you would on your holiday home. You will also be paying rates, land tax and other costs on your holiday home, which could add up to at least another $1000.

This all means you are forgoing $4000 to $8500 in after-tax income each year. A family of four could have a quite respectable seaside holiday once or twice a year for $4000, $8500 would buy a holiday in Europe or a trip to Disneyland. You may decide that you prefer the holiday home to the hassle of booking trips and staying at hotels. This is fine. Just keep in mind the alternatives.

Residential rental property

Residential rental property does not give you a fantastic return on your money—usually not more than 4 per cent before tax, after you have paid the managing agent and paid for council rates, land tax and repairs. However, you will get the capital appreciation and, overall, you will do better than you will with a holiday home that you don't rent out.

If you have trouble letting the house, or you get problem tenants, the return could be much lower. You also have the hassles associated with owning a house, like painting, mending leaking roofs, controlling pests, replacing hot water systems and other such problems.

If you are paying outright for a rental house, buy it in the name of the lower income earning partner. This may make a large difference to the tax you pay on the rental income and the CGT when you sell. If you are borrowing the money for the rental house, and the interest payments and other costs are higher than the rental income, buy it in the name of the higher income earning partner. At the time of writing the loss can be deducted from your normal salary and a tax rebate claimed. We will cover this further a bit later, under negative gearing.

If you own your own home, you know by now what to look for when buying homes, and it is fun looking around to buy a house. It can also be fun doing up houses. If you buy investment property you can have these benefits without the bother of moving house.

Property returns

Residential property returns are usually quoted on the increase in median prices of homes in an area. Sometimes only a few homes were actually sold during the year. The average home has become larger and better fitted out over the years that the figures have been kept and this median price increase does not take into account the fact that houses are improved as time goes on, particularly in better suburbs. This improvement cost becomes part of the increase in the median value but it is not profit. Median values also disregard the considerable costs of buying and selling houses, with agents' fees and stamp duty. These costs can easily amount to 5 per cent to 10 per cent of the original cost of the home. This could reduce a claimed 20 per cent gain by half.

On the other hand, this measure is only the increase in the price of homes. It does not include the rental return you receive if you rent the house out.

Commercial property

Buying commercial property is generally out of reach of individual investors, unless you buy one or two small units, or join a syndicate. The returns are good if your units are leased, not so good otherwise.

Unless you are really into commercial property, you are best buying into commercial property trusts. These generally have a large property base, top companies as tenants, a high average tenancy and a knowledgeable manager. Do not invest large amounts of your retirement money in any one trust. Never forget that rule number one is to diversify.

Sharemarket

The sharemarket will normally give you the best overall return on your savings over the long term.

Some people think the sharemarket is only for experts and others think it is only for gamblers, but more and more

Australians own shares. Anyone can understand enough about the sharemarket to invest safely. Buying blue-chip shares and holding them for long lengths of time is a safe way to make a respectable amount of money. You don't have to be a day-trader or buy options or futures to make money from the sharemarket.

How the sharemarket works

In Australia, companies can be private or public, and public companies can be listed or unlisted. Private companies are normally owned by an individual, a family, or a group of people. Unlisted public companies are owned by a group of shareholders or another company. Listed public companies are owned by shareholders and anyone can buy shares in any listed public company. A stock exchange is a market where shareholders can buy or sell their shares. At the time of writing, there are around 1400 companies listed on the Australian Stock Exchange (ASX).

Most public companies started life as private companies. Changing from a private company to a public company is called floating the company. The owners of the company offer some or all of their shares for sale to the public, and they may issue additional shares to raise more capital for expansion or to retire debt.

With the privatisation of public utilities, such as Telstra, the government gets the money that the shareholders pay to buy the shares.

Directors

Shareholders are the owners of the company although they are not involved in the day-to-day management. The company is run by directors, who oversee the management and represent the interests of the shareholders. Directors are normally appointed by the shareholders at the annual general meeting (AGM) of the company.

Dividends

The company profits can be paid out to the shareholders as dividends or retained by the company to pay debts or fund further expansion.

Companies pay tax on their profits before the profit is distributed to shareholders as a dividend. The shareholder then has to pay income tax on the dividend. To avoid the amount being taxed twice, the shareholder is given a tax credit for the tax paid by the company and this credit reduces the tax owed by the shareholder. This is called a franking credit or imputation credit.

Most dividends are franked; that is, the tax has already been paid by the company. You are paid the dividend in cash and given a value for the franking credit. Both the dividend and the franking credit are part of your taxable income, but the amount of the franking credit reduces the amount of tax that you owe. Excess franking credits are now refundable by the ATO.

For example, if you receive a dividend for $70, with a franking credit of $30, you will receive the $70 in cash. When you come to fill in your tax return, you add the $70 dividend and the $30 credit to give $100 of income. Your tax will be calculated on the $100, but the amount of tax you owe will be then reduced by the $30. If you are on the lowest marginal tax rate of 18.5 per cent, then you will be assessed for $18.50 in tax and the remaining $11.50 of the $30 tax credit will be refunded to you by the ATO. If you are on the top tax rate

(48.5 per cent) you will owe $48.50 in tax, less the $30 credit, so you will need to pay the ATO a further $18.50.

Some companies allow you to reinvest your dividend in extra shares in the company, usually at a small discount to the current market price. You still have to declare the dividend as income and you can still use the franking credit. The company benefits by having a continual supply of extra capital for expansion or debt reduction.

Buying and selling shares

Once a company has been floated, shareholders can sell their shares to someone else on the ASX. Shares are valued by investors according to the value of the assets the company owns, the dividends that the company is paying and the prospect of future growth in company earnings.

To buy and sell shares you need to go through a stockbroker and you will pay brokerage charges, usually around 2 per cent with a $100 minimum. This can be reduced to 1 per cent with a $50 minimum if you go through a discount stockbroker, and around $20 or less if you trade over the Internet. A discount stockbroker will execute your orders, but will not give you advice on which shares to buy as a normal stockbroker will.

Most stockbrokers now have an Internet site and many brokers will allow you to trade shares online. There are lots of sites with free information about companies and share prices, and forums to exchange news and ideas on which stocks to buy. Do a search on 'Australian sharemarket' to find current web addresses.

Shares have the advantages over property that they don't need painting, weeding or other maintenance and you don't have problems with tenants. You can buy or sell shares in smaller amounts and much more quickly and easily than you can houses. They have the advantages over fixed interest investments that your returns are higher on average, particularly after tax, and part of your return is in capital growth. And shares are much more interesting than managed funds. They really can be fun!

Shares have the disadvantage that you can look up their current value at any time. Yes, I did say disadvantage. If they are worth less than you paid, you know about it. You can't decide on the exact value of an investment property just by looking at a newspaper, but you can with shares, and they are much more likely to go down over short periods of time than property values are.

Many small investors who go into the sharemarket don't realise just how volatile share prices can be. Sharemarket books are always full of optimism, vast returns, easy profits and graphs that climb steeply upwards.

Share prices of individual companies do fall at times, and companies occasionally fail altogether. At the time of writing, both HIH Insurance and Harris Scarfe Holdings are in liquidation and shareholders appear unlikely to get any of their money back. Neither of these companies would have been considered a particularly high-risk investment in the weeks before they failed. If you invest in the sharemarket, diversifying your investments is very, very important. If you had all of your money in HIH Insurance, you may have lost the lot. If you had 5 per cent of your money in this company, this would have been a setback, but not a major disaster. I had a few hundred dollars in HIH Insurance when it failed. This was only a very small fraction of my total sharemarket investment. An investor I know lost one-third of the money in his self-managed super fund. It may take him several years to get back to where he was. The loss was a minor one for me, but a major one for my friend.

There are a lot of excellent books on the sharemarket, and there are various strategies for making money. Read all you can about sharemarket investing before you take the plunge. You need to be familiar with sharemarket terms and investing and trading strategies.

If you like the idea of sharemarket investing, but don't have the confidence to pick shares yourself, you can invest in a listed investment company (LIC). These are covered in more detail in the next section.

Managed investments

If you do not want to invest directly in either property or shares yourself, managed investments are the perfect answer to diversifying your risk and increasing your returns without a lot of work or worry.

Most super funds are just managed investments that look after superannuation money rather than normal savings. You can put savings into managed investments just like you put super into super funds.

How they work

Managed investments involve a lot of people paying in small amounts of money to a fund or trust, which then invests the resulting large amount of money in a range of shares, property, bonds and other investments. An experienced fund manager makes all the investment decisions, your money is spread over a range of investments, and all you need to do is bank the dividend when the statement arrives.

When you buy units in a trust, you pay a price per unit that varies from day to day, or week to week, and reflects the current value of the assets of the trust. This value goes up over the years, so as well as receiving dividends from your trust, your units will go up in value. This increase in value will be a capital gain when you sell your units.

You buy your units in the fund at a price representing the total net assets of the fund divided by the total number of units at the time you buy the units. This is the net asset backing per unit. Your money is added to the assets of the trust and used to buy more shares or property or whatever the fund specialises in. If you want your money back, you get an amount per unit equivalent to the net asset backing per unit at the time of redemption of your units. This may be more or less than you paid depending on the current value of the fund's assets.

The trust will take a small percentage of the annual income to cover the costs of running the trust and paying the manager. This is normally around 1.5 per cent to 2 per cent. The returns are normally quoted after this fee is taken out. This is called the management expense ratio (MER).

Check the up-front fees before you invest in a trust, and any exit fees. If you arrange your investments through a financial planner, the trust may take out 4 per cent of your original investment and pay it to the financial planner as a commission. So for every $1000 you invest, you only get $960 worth of units. There are, however, specialist discount investment brokers, who will refund most of the up-front fee if you invest in the trust through them. The 4 per cent commission is worth saving.

Most discount brokers have Internet websites and you can order a managed fund prospectus online. The broker's name will be stamped on your application form and the fund will give you more units instead of paying the broker's commission. So what is in it for the discount broker? Sometimes they get a small up-front commission, say 0.5 per cent of your funds instead of 4 per cent, and sometimes they get a small trailing commission on the amount you invest, paid by the fund manager, not by you.

Trusts often have a spread between the entry price for units and the exit price for units. This is usually not more than about 0.5 per cent. This is supposed to protect investors who invest in the fund for the long term from the costs incurred by the fund on investors who buy and sell units frequently.

You can generally have your dividend reinvested in more units in your trust. This is excellent for your retirement plan. Keep the records for calculating your tax as the dividend amount is taxable. This is all you have to do.

In a market crash, property price slump or a panic sell-off by investors, the managed fund may run out of cash to pay to investors wanting to redeem their units. The fund may be obliged to sell some of the assets of the fund at low prices to pay back the investors. This can result in the unit price going even lower and more investors wanting to take their money out. All funds keep sufficient cash to cover most panic situations and, in times of panic selling, they will sometimes halt the buying and selling of units until the crisis is over.

If some of your investments don't make a good return every year, don't worry unduly about it. Most investment funds make money most years. But there will be years when some funds go backwards, even the best funds. On average, over ten or twenty years, your returns will be excellent.

Types of trusts

There are different types of unit trusts, depending whether the money is invested in shares, property or fixed interest securities such as bonds. Some funds have a mixture of various proportions of these three. Balanced funds, for example, normally have around 30 per cent of their money in shares, with the remainder in fixed interest securities and property. Growth funds usually have around 70 per cent of their money invested in shares. Some funds specialise in Australian investments, some in overseas investments and some in a mixture of these. All funds keep some of their money in cash, so they can repay investors who want to sell their units.

The mix of investments for each fund type is usually explained in the prospectus. Don't be daunted by the choices. If you are not sure which fund is best for you, contact the financial institution. They will be happy to advise you on this.

You may want to spread your investments over different types of funds as well as over different financial institutions.

Listed trusts

Some trusts are listed on the sharemarket. These generally specialise in either property or shares, rather than a mix. Trusts specialising in property are called listed property trusts and those investing in shares are called listed investment companies.

If you buy and sell shares in listed companies you pay only the brokerage. There are no other entry or exit fees. You can keep track of listed trusts on the Internet or in the sharemarket tables published in daily newspapers, and it is quick and easy to buy and sell your shares.

Listed trusts usually have a smaller management expense

ratio than managed funds, as they simply look after the funds under their control and don't need to advertise for new investors or continually process new investment money coming in or investors wanting to redeem their units for cash.

Another advantage of listed trusts is that in a panic sell-off by shareholders, the share price will go down, but the trust will not be obliged to sell assets at low prices. The trust has no obligation to pay back the shareholders. If you keep your shares and wait for better times they will go back up again and meanwhile, for property trusts the tenants are still paying rent, and for share trusts the companies are still paying dividends, so you will still get your dividend from the listed trust.

The only disadvantage is that there are far fewer listed trusts than managed funds, so your choice of investment is not as great. You can, for example, invest in a managed fund specialising in European shares, but there is currently no listed trust with only European shares.

Lazy investing

If you are not confident about choosing your own investments, if picking your own investments doesn't appeal to you, or if you don't want to take the time to do some research, then invest your money in a managed fund run by your bank.

Most funds have a savings plan, allowing you to automatically invest a fixed amount each month. You can set-and-forget your retirement plan by arranging to have the payment you used to make on your mortgage put into the fund each month.

The bank will advise you on the type of fund that is best for you, depending on how long it will be before you retire.

This advice from a bank is generally free. Your money will be invested over a range of fixed interest securities, property, and Australian and overseas shares by a fund manager who is an investment expert. You will probably pay an up-front commission to the bank, but this is the price of not doing your own research.

You may want to diversify by having some of your funds in similar investments with other banks or large financial institutions. Although you are unlikely to lose your money in a fund manged by a major bank, some fund managers do better than others and this may vary from year to year.

Super or non-super savings

You will also need to decide how much of your money you put into superannuation and how much you save yourself outside of the super system.

You should already have some money in super that your employer is obliged to contribute for you. This amount is called the superannuation guarantee. This will be equivalent to 9 per cent of your pay by 2003. You may also contribute some of your own after-tax funds to super and your employer may also put in additional employer contributions for you.

Super should be the cornerstone of everyone's retirement savings. Don't ignore super as a means of saving money because it is so complex, or because it doesn't seem tangible to you when you can't access it until you retire. But on the other hand, don't blindly pour all of your savings into super in the hope you will retire a millionaire. You may get a surprise bill from the tax department when you come to claim the million dollars.

Superannuation basics

Superannuation has become ridiculously complex and is perceived as such, so that most people just contribute blindly with no idea of whether they would be better off investing the money themselves. Understand the basics and make super work for you. Most of the complication is only in the detail, and much of it involves old rules, which may have predated your contributions. Read some up-to-date books on super so you understand how it works and how it can benefit you.

The basics of how superannuation works for most employees are:

- While you are employed you pay some of your money into a fund with less tax to pay than if you received the extra as income. The tax is 15 per cent for most people.
- If you have an income above around $85 000 including the value of super contributions paid by your employer you may have to pay a higher rate of tax on your employer contributions. This can increase to 30 per cent for total incomes over around $100 000. This extra tax is called the superannuation surcharge. The income amounts where the surcharge starts to apply are indexed each year.
- Your money is invested for you until you retire with a tax rate of 15 per cent on the investment earnings.
- You take your money when you retire either as a cash payment or as an income stream.
- If you take your money as an income stream, you pay normal rates of income tax on it, with a rebate of 15 per cent to allow for the tax you paid when the money entered the fund. If your marginal rate of tax is 31.5 per cent after

your retirement, you will be paying 16.5 per cent tax on your income.

- If you take your money as a cash payment (called a lump sum), then you normally pay tax at 16.5 per cent on the amount above around $100 000. This amount is called the low-rate threshold and it is indexed each year.
- There is an upper limit on the amount of super that can be saved tax effectively. This upper limit is called the reasonable benefit limit (RBL) and it is indexed each year. It is around $507 000 at the time of writing. Any after-tax money that you put into super yourself is not included in the RBL amount.
- If your super payout is above the RBL, you will pay the top marginal rate of tax on the amount above the RBL (called the excess component), if you want to retain control over it. This is in addition to the 15 per cent you already paid (or 30 per cent if you pay the full superannuation surcharge).
- If you don't want to pay this extra tax on the excess component, you can put it into a life annuity, where you give your funds to an insurance company in exchange for a fixed income for the remainder of your life. The income may have a 15 per cent rebate attached, but does not always attract this rebate.

The basic advantage of super is that you pay less tax on the income the fund is earning for you, however, with lower income tax rates super is not as attractive as it once was. The basic disadvantages are that you don't have access to the money until you retire, and when you do retire, you pay tax on your super and lose a lot of the original benefit.

Here is a brief summary of the advantages and disadvantages of superannuation.

Advantages of super

- The earnings of the super fund are taxed at only 15 per cent. If this money was in non-super savings, you could be paying up to 48.5 per cent of the earnings in tax.
- The earnings on your super are not added to your taxable income for calculating superannuation surcharge or welfare benefits.
- Employer contributions are taxed at 15 per cent when they are put into super. For high-income earners, this can be up to 30 per cent, but it is still less than the marginal rate of tax.
- The money is preserved, so you cannot access it until you reach retiring age. You cannot be tempted into spending it.
- Super paid by your employer as salary sacrifice is a very good deal indeed, unless it will take your total benefit over the RBL.
- If you take your payment as a lump sum, rather than converting it to a pension or annuity, the first $100 000 or so (at the time of writing) is tax free, so you pay only the original 15 per cent (or up to 30 per cent with the surcharge) on this amount. This low-rate threshold is indexed each year.

Disadvantages of super

- If the rules are changed so that super is no longer tax effective for you, you cannot take your money out. Even after-tax contributions you make yourself are now preserved.
- If you want to retire early, you cannot access your super.
- Your super is usually under the control of one fund manager. You cannot diversify your super to anywhere near the degree you can diversify non-super savings.

- Unless you take your super payout as a lump sum, and pay extra tax on it, you cannot split your super between partners when you retire to minimise the tax on the income. (At the time of writing, however, there are plans to change this).
- The 15 per cent tax when you put your money into super is not the end of the story. When you retire, you will pay either lump sum tax if you take your payout as a cash lump sum, or income tax if it is paid back to you as a pension or income stream.
- If your super payout is higher than the RBL, then you may be paying a whacking total tax rate on that part of your super payout. This can be up to 78.5 per cent of your money in some circumstances.
- Super is under the control of government rules, which can be changed at whim. Savings outside the super system are totally under your control.

Choosing the balance

You have to weigh up the tax benefits against the loss of control of your money. Almost everyone will benefit by having a super payout of the low-rate threshold, currently around $100 000. This amount is indexed each year. However, many people will have this amount from the superannuation guarantee amount put in by their employer.

If you are not a high-income earner (in the top income tax bracket), you should be able to contribute around 5 per cent of your gross pay to super without exceeding the RBL.

Try to equalise the amount of super between partners. You can contribute to your partner's fund rather than your own, and you may get a tax rebate for this. Having two lots of super will allow you to retire with two tax-free amounts and two RBL amounts between you. It will also give you two similar incomes when you retire. This is more tax effective than one partner receiving most of the income.

Low-income earners fare much better than high-income earners on the money they save outside the super system, as they pay less tax on the earnings. The tax system is actually stacked to favour low-income earners over high-income earners where savings income is concerned, because low-income earners keep more of their interest and dividends.

Salary sacrifice

If you are on one of the top two tax brackets, or if you are currently making employee contributions to super, you may like to consider salary sacrifice, as this is a very efficient way to save for your retirement. We talked a bit about salary sacrifice in Chapter 3.

It works like this. Instead of paying all your salary to you, your employer pays some of it directly to your super fund as an employer contribution. If money is paid to you, you pay tax on it at your marginal rate. If it is paid into the super fund as an employer contribution the tax taken out is only 15 per cent for most people, or up to 30 per cent if you have a high income and pay the full superannuation surcharge. So more of your money is left after tax for investment in the fund.

Let's look at an example. Suppose you are on the top tax rate, currently 48.5 per cent. Of the top $1000 of your pay, you get to keep $515 and $485 goes in tax. If you invest this money yourself, you will be putting $515 into the investment and paying tax at the top rate on your investment income.

However, if your employer pays you $1000 less in salary, and puts that money straight into superannuation as an employer contribution, then the tax is usually $150, leaving $850 to be invested by the fund on your behalf. Even if you pay the full surcharge, the tax is a maximum of $300, leaving $700 to invest. The tax on the fund earnings is only 15 per cent, so your fund keeps more of your investment income than you would investing yourself.

You may pay some additional tax when you retire and take your super, but meanwhile the extra money has been earning interest and compounding much more quickly than if you had invested outside the super system.

Salary sacrifice works best for employees who are earning enough to be in the top tax bracket, but earning less than the threshold for the superannuation surcharge. But even outside this range, it is still effective.

If you are putting your own money into super as an employee contribution, you are better off with salary sacrifice even if you are on the normal 31.5 per cent tax rate. Not all employers will allow you to take income as salary sacrifice, but if you feel it will benefit you, ask if you have the option.

Diversifying your super

Try to diversify your super if you possibly can. If you leave a job and have a rollover amount, don't automatically put it in your new employer's fund. Put the money in a rollover fund with a bank or another financial institution. Then you will have two fund managers looking after your money, one for the rollover and one for the super you get from your new employer. If one fund does poorly, chances are the other one will do better.

Keep in mind that if your super is all in one fund, you are relying heavily on the investment success of one organisation and probably one fund manager. Unless you have changed employment several times and were able to roll over your super into several different funds that you have selected yourself, it is difficult to diversify your super over different fund managers and organisations.

Even with the introduction of choice of funds, the choices may still be very limited. You may still be obliged to have your entire super with one fund manager. By the time you retire, your super may be worth several hundred thousand dollars, and if the fund does poorly just before you retire, you will never have the opportunity to save that money again. Diversify your super as much as you can.

Tax on investments

Investment income is taxed just like any other income, although some investment types have special tax treatment. If you fill in your own tax return, follow the instructions for where to put interest and dividend income and income from property trusts. Property trusts send their investors a tax statement at the end of the financial year with detailed instructions on how to deal with the various amounts. If you have your tax return done for you, just keep all the statements you receive and hand them to your tax agent.

You can normally claim as a deduction any legitimate costs involved in earning your investment income, including investment magazines and costs involved in attending company meetings.

Capital gains tax

If you make a profit when you sell shares or residential real estate, you will need to pay capital gains tax (CGT) on the difference between the price you paid, including all purchase costs, and the price you receive, less any selling costs. We will call this the net gain. The amount of CGT you pay depends on when you purchased the asset and how long you held it.

The ATO have some excellent booklets available on CGT. If you invest in anything more complex than fixed interest investments, contact the ATO and ask them to send you the CGT information.

A brief outline of the rules for CGT at the time of writing is:

- for assets purchased prior to 20 September 1985, CGT does not apply;
- for assets purchased and sold within one year, you pay tax on the net gain at your normal marginal rate—this is referred to by the ATO as the 'other method';
- for assets purchased after 21 September 1999 and held for more than one year, you pay tax at your marginal rate on half of the net gain—this is called the 'discount method'; and
- for assets purchased between 20 September 1985 and 21 September 1999, you can choose the discount method or the older indexation method. For the indexation method, you index the cost base for changes in the Consumer Price index before calculating the net gain. You will need to obtain the CGT booklet from the ATO for detailed instructions on how to index a cost base.

Gearing investments

Gearing is borrowing money and investing it at a higher overall rate of return, so you gain investment income and profit without needing money of your own. We spoke a bit about gearing investments in the section on borrowing for investments (see p 86).

If you borrow $100 000 at 7 per cent and invest it at 8 per cent, then you are making $1000 per year without any outlay of your own money at all. Gearing only works if the total return in income and capital gain is higher than the interest rate on the money you borrow.

For most conventional geared investments, you will need to put down a deposit on your asset, usually 20 per cent for property and 30 per cent for shares.

Here is an example of gearing for a sharemarket investment in a company that does very well, doubling in price over the course of a year. In the first instance you buy the shares with $35 000 of your own money. In the second instance you put in $30 000 of your own money and $70 000 of borrowed money. The interest rate is 7 per cent and you pay $100 loan costs, so your total interest payment is $5000. In both instances you have put in $35 000 of your own money.

At the end of the year you sell the shares for twice what you paid. In the first case, you receive $70 000 and have made $35 000 profit. In the second case, you receive $200 000 and pay the bank back their $70 000, leaving you with your original $35 000 and $95 000 profit.

In the first case, you have made a 100 per cent return on your investment, but in the second case, you have made around 270 per cent return. This increase in the return is why this is called gearing. This is illustrated in Table 6.2.

Gearing can go wrong

You gain a greater return on your money if you gear investments and make a profit than if you buy an asset with your

Table 6.2 Example of gearing

	Non-geared	Geared
Your money	$35 000	$30 000
Interest paid	—	$5000
Loan money	—	$70 000
Cost of shares	$35 000	$100 000
Investment sold	$70 000	$200 000
Profit	$35 000	$95 000
Profit %	100%	271%

own money. Gearing relies on the total return of income and capital gain being higher than the interest rate at which you borrow the money. It magnifies the return on your money by allowing you to make a larger profit with a small investment of your own funds.

Gearing can work the other way, however, and magnify your losses. In the example above, let us suppose that the company whose shares you bought went broke and you lost the lot.

In the first case, you have lost all your money. Your loss is 100 per cent. In the second case you have lost all you borrowed and the interest you paid as well as your original $30 000. You still have to pay back the loan. You have lost $105 000, which is 300 per cent of your $35 000 investment.

If you borrow money to buy shares, you can normally only borrow 70 per cent of the value of your shares. If the share price drops, the lender will ask you to pay back some of the loan so it is still only 70 per cent of the new value of the shares. This is called a margin call. If you cannot pay the extra, the lender will sell some of your shares (at the lower current price) to cover the margin. You don't have the opportunity to sit tight until the share price recovers. If you borrow to buy shares, you can lose money fast in a sharemarket crash.

Negative gearing

If you borrow money to invest, and the income from the investment is less than the interest rate, but you are relying on capital gain to make a profit, then you are negative gearing your investment. You are making a loss while you hold the asset in expectation of a capital gain when you sell.

At the time of writing you can usually claim the loss as a tax deduction against your normal income and receive a tax rebate. This reduces the effect of the loss while you own the asset. When you sell the asset, you make a capital gain and ultimately make a profit (hopefully!).

Negative gearing is used extensively (but not exclusively) for investing in residential rental property, where the rental return does not fully cover the costs involved. You can claim a tax deduction for some non-cash expenses, such as depreciation on the building and the fittings, and your tax rebate allows for this amount, so your actual negative cashflow may be quite small.

There are some excellent books available on negative gearing residential property. If this idea appeals to you, look into it further.

Some investors negative gear shares, where the dividend income does not fully cover the cost of borrowing the money. You gain on the capital appreciation of the shares when you come to sell them.

Putting it all together

In summary, here are some of the main guidelines for planning your investments:

- saving 10 per cent of your take-home pay over your lifetime will give you a decent retirement income;
- using this 10 per cent to fast-track your mortgage then investing the total amount you were paying off your mortgage will allow you to retire with an even better income;
- take advantage of the tax concessions of superannuation if this benefits you;
- diversify your savings over fixed interest, property and shares;
- diversify your sharemarket and managed fund investments so that you have at most 10 per cent of your total in any one company, fund or project;
- if you have a partner, aim to retire with two lots of super, invest your savings in the name of the lower income partner, and rearrange your investments to split your income equally after you retire; and
- understand your investments, and learn everything you can about investing.

Keeping ahead of change

Mortgage rates, offset accounts, bank products, tax rules, super rules and investment products are all constantly changing. You need to keep up with these changes to make the most of your money.

Think ahead when you choose your mortgage and your investments. Could you still afford the repayments on your home loan if interest rates went up? Would you be happy to be locked into a five-year term deposit at 5 per cent if by next year the rates were 8 per cent?

Before you go into long-term investments, think about the results of changes to the tax rules and changes to your circumstances. Don't get locked into long-term schemes that you can't get out of without losing money.

Be prepared to change banks if another bank can give you a better return or a more convenient account type. (But don't go to the trouble of changing banks for small gains.) If you need a loan, ask for details from all the banks, not just your usual one. Look at less obvious sources of finance, such as mortgage providers, smaller banks, building societies or credit unions.

Think about the return on your savings when you invest your money. Changes in the home loan rate may make it more or less attractive to put all of your money into paying off your mortgage, rather than into other investments.

Read everything you can about investing your money. Most people are perfectly capable of running their own financial affairs. No one else can look after your interests better than you can if you take the trouble to keep informed.

If things go a little wrong sometimes, don't worry and keep going. If you spend more than you should occasionally and can't make an extra mortgage payment, if you need to spend some of your retirement money in a family disaster, if an investment goes horribly wrong and you lose some of your savings, just pick up the pieces and keep going on.

While you are paying off your mortgage, think in terms of how far you have come already, not how much further you have to go. When you have paid off your mortgage, celebrate your first milestone and start to save for your retirement. Your savings may seem to grow very slowly to start with, but to retire wealthy you don't need to be rich by tomorrow. Enjoy counting how much you have saved and planning how much you will save.

Abbreviations

ASX	Australian Stock Exchange
ATM	Automatic teller machine
ATO	Australian Tax Office
CGT	Capital gains tax
EFTPOS	Electronic funds transfer at point of sale
GDT	Government debits tax
HECS	Higher Education Contribution Scheme
LIC	Listed investment company
MER	Management expense ratio
Misa	Mortgage interest saver account
RBL	Reasonable benefit limit

Glossary

Bridging finance An interest only loan allowing you to borrow money to buy a house while you are waiting to sell your current home, or waiting for some other large payment.

Brokerage An amount charged by a dealer in securities (usually a stockbroker) to buy and sell shares, bank bills or other investment products for you.

Budget loan A home loan with a lower interest rate but with fewer bells and whistles than a standard loan.

Cash management account A savings account with a high rate of interest that you can use for large sums of money. You will normally need to keep a minimum of $5000 in your account.

Conveyancing Conveyancing is the actual transfer of the title of your home to your name, and the payment to the vendor of your deposit and the loan amount from the bank. This is usually done by a solicitor or a settlement agent.

Dividend An amount paid each year to shareholders by a company in return for the shareholder investing in the company. The dividend is normally a distribution of the profits that the company has made that year. Most companies pay dividends twice a year.

Fixed rate loan A loan where the interest rate is fixed for the first one to five years of the loan. This allows you to plan your finances ahead, as you know exactly what your repayments will be for the term of the loan and you will not be affected by interest rate rises.

Franking credit Companies pay tax on their profit before it is distributed to shareholders as a dividend. The shareholder then has to pay income tax on the dividend. To avoid the amount being taxed twice, the shareholder is given a tax credit for the tax paid by the company and this credit reduces the tax owed by the shareholder. Also called imputation credit.

Gearing and negative gearing Gearing is borrowing money and investing it at a higher rate of return, so you gain investment income and profit without using money of your own. If you borrow money to invest, and the income from the investment is less than the interest rate, but you are relying on capital gain to make a profit, then you are negative gearing your investment.

Government debits tax Government debits tax (GDT) is a tax levied on every withdrawal from a bank account with a cheque facility. This tax is due to be phased out in 2005.

Home equity loan A loan set up as a line of credit, similar to a bank overdraft, allowing you to make payments then take all or part of your money back out. Interest is calculated on the daily balance, so you only pay interest on the amount outstanding.

Honeymoon rate A special fixed lower interest rate charged for the first year of your loan.

Inflation The purchasing power of your money reduces over time due to rising costs and rising wages. This effect is called inflation and can be measured by increases in the price of everyday items and the average cost of living for families.

Interest only loan A loan where your payment amount only covers the interest on the amount borrowed, so you never pay the loan off.

Keycard account A day-to-day bank account with a debit card that you can use for withdrawing cash and paying for purchases.

Liquidity Liquidity is the ease with which you can convert your investments to cash. Cash in the bank is the most liquid of assets, followed by shares, with property the most difficult to convert to cash.

Loan set-up fee An up-front fee charged by the bank for setting up your loan, checking your credentials and valuing the property you are buying. The fee is typically around $600, but the bank may waive it entirely in some circumstances.

Managed investments Managed investments involve a lot of people paying in small amounts of money to a fund or trust, which then invests the resulting large amount of money in a range of shares, property, bonds and other investments. An experienced fund manager chooses the investments.

Misa account A Misa (mortgage interest saver) account is an offset account with either an offset rate less than the mortgage rate, or a small minimum withdrawal fee (typically $100) or both of these features.

Mortgage broker A mortgage broker can arrange your loan for you with the institution he or she feels will give you the best deal. The broker receives commission from the lending institution.

Mortgage insurance An insurance policy taken out by the bank at your expense to cover any shortfall if you default on your loan payments and they are obliged to sell your home to get their money back.

Offset account A bank account where the interest the bank pays on your money is paid into your home loan instead of being paid to you directly.

Principal and interest loan A loan where your repayment amount covers the interest and part of the principal, so the loan is eventually paid out.

Reasonable benefit limit The maximum amount of superannuation you can accumulate without having an excess component. The excess component is taxed very heavily if you want to take your super as a cash benefit or a normal superannuation pension when you retire. This amount includes your employer contributions and the earnings of the fund, but not any after-tax money you invested yourself in super.

Redraw account A redraw account or redraw facility allows you to make extra lump sum payments off your loan, then withdraw the extra money later if you need it.

Salary account An offset account with full offset and no minimum deposit or withdrawal amount. Normally you can use a salary account for your day-to-day banking.

Salary sacrifice A scheme by which your employer pays part of your salary into your super fund instead of paying it to you. This results in less tax being taken from the money, so more of your money is invested.

Stamp duty A tax paid to your state or territory government on land transfers and on mortgages.

Superannuation guarantee A set percentage of an employee's wage that an employer is obliged to pay into a super fund for the employee. The rate is 8 per cent at the time of writing, but will rise to 9 per cent by 2003.

Superannuation surcharge If the total of your income and your employer superannuation contributions is above a certain amount, currently around $85 000, then your employer contributions to super are taxed at a higher rate than the normal 15 per cent. This higher rate phases in over an income range and can be as high as 30 per cent. This extra tax is called the superannuation surcharge. The income amounts where the surcharge starts to apply are indexed each year.

Term deposit Most banks offer term deposits, allowing you to invest large sums of money for a set number of months or years at a set interest rate. A term deposit normally gives you a better return than a savings account.

Variable rate loan A loan where the interest rate varies from time to time with current market rates. Your repayment amount will vary with the interest rate.

Vendor The person selling a home is called the vendor. The person buying is called the purchaser.

Useful websites

Internet website addresses can change quite rapidly. This list was current at the time of writing and is by no means exhaustive. For current home loan websites, do an Internet search on 'home loan' and 'Australia'. For mortgage brokers try 'mortgage broker' and 'Australia'. Some search engines will allow you to confine the search to Australian sites.

If you visit my homepage you will find a current list of mortgage websites and you can download the spreadsheets and tables from this book. The address is:

www.lainie.com.au

Banks

Adelaide Bank	www.adelaidebank.com.au
ANZ Bank	www.anz.com.au
Bank of South Australia	www.banksa.com.au
Bankwest	www.bankwest.com.au
Commonwealth Bank	www.commbank.com.au
St George Bank	www.stgeorge.com.au
National Australia Bank	www.national.com.au
Westpac Bank	www.westpac.com.au

Suncorp Metway	www.suncorpmetway.com.au
Bendigo Bank	www.bendigobank.com.au
The Rock Building Society	www.therock.com.au
Homepath (CBA)	www.homepath.com.au

Credit unions

Police and Nurses Credit Society	www.pncs.com.au
Circle Credit	www.circle.com.au
Prospect Credit Union	www.prospectcu.com.au
Credit Union Australia	www.cua.com.au

Non-bank lenders

Austral Online	www.austral.com.au
Direct Home Loans	www.directhomeloans.com.au
RAMS	www.rams.com.au
AIMS Home Loans	www.aimshomeloans.com.au
Wizard	www.ewizard.com.au
Aussie Home Loans	www.aussiehomeloans.com.au
The Better Mortgage Company	www.bmcloans.com.au
Homeloans Limited	www.homeloans.com.au

Mortgage brokers

Mr Mortgage	www.mrmortgage.com.au
Mortgage Choice	www.mortgagechoice.com.au
Iconex Home Loans	www.iconexhomeloans.com.au
Smartline Home Loans	www.smartline.com.au
Johnson Taylor Potter	www.jtpmp.com.au
The Mortgage Store	www.mortgagestore.com.au

Other useful sites

Homestart	www.homestart.com.au
Keystart	www.keystart.com.au

First Home Buyers Scheme	www.firsthome.gov.au
Money Manager	www.moneymanager.com.au
Australian Taxation Office	www.ato.gov.au

Spreadsheets and calculations

Here are the instructions for writing your own mortgage spreadsheet. I have also given instructions for setting this up approximately using a calculator. Remember all calculations in this book are optional. The method of fast-tracking your mortgage then saving for your retirement will work even if you never calculate anything.

Most families these days have a home computer, and the instructions are quite detailed, so even if you have never used a spreadsheet program before, you can learn as you go. The most common spreadsheet program is Excel. If you are using a different program, Lotus 123 for example, there may be some small differences in the syntax.

If at any time you feel you are out of your depth, then use the tables at the back of this book instead.

You can download the mortgage spreadsheet (and all the other worksheets) used in this book from my webpage. You can then substitute the values for your own mortgage in the downloaded worksheet. See the Useful Websites section for my webpage address.

Spreadsheet basics

If you have never used a spreadsheet program on a computer before, don't worry. Just open the program and follow the instructions. Spreadsheets are incredibly useful, and once you get to know how to use them, you will find yourself using them for all sorts of applications.

The cells are named with the letter at the top of the column and the number at the left of the row. So the top left-hand cell is called A1 and the third cell in the first row is called C1. Each cell of the worksheet can contain text, a number, or a formula or function to do a calculation. A formula is just an arithmetic expression, and a function is a shortcut way to do a calculation.

A formula or function starts with = in Excel. This is how the program knows it's a formula or function and not just text. **Please note that there are no spaces in any formulas or functions. I have added spaces only to make it easier to read.**

If you put the number 1 in cell A1, the number 2 in cell B1 and in C1 put the formula:

= A1 + B1

your spreadsheet will have the number 3 displayed in C1. If you change the number in cell A1 to 5, then C1 will automatically change to display 7.

If you copy and paste cells within a worksheet, the program will automatically update the cell references for you. Select what you want to copy and select **Edit → Copy**. Then select the cell or range of cells you want to paste to and select **Edit → Paste.**

If you now put the number 3 in A2 and the number 5 in B2 and copy the formula from C1 to C2, the formula in C2 will read:

= A2 + B2

and the number displayed in C2 will be 8.

If you don't want the references to update when you copy, for example if you were adding a number stored in cell A1 to a column of numbers in B1 to B6, you need to anchor the reference by using a $ sign before the column or row number or both.

Put the number 2 in cell A1 and the numbers 1 to 6 in B1 to B6. Now in C1 put the formula:

= B1 + $A$1

then copy this cell to cells C2 to C6. C1 to C6 will now display the numbers 3 to 8.

A function is a shortcut way of doing a more complex calculation. You write the name of the function, and the cells or numbers you are working on in brackets after it. Don't leave a space between the function name and the bracket.

If you need to refer to a whole range of cells, use the top left-hand reference and the bottom right-hand reference with a colon between them.

This is a formula that adds all the numbers in a row:

= A1 + B1 + C1 + D1 + E1 + F1

You can instead use the SUM function to get the same result:

= SUM(A1: F1)

The arithmetic symbols used for worksheets are:

Add	+
Subtract	–
Multiply	*
Divide	/
Raise to power	^

To calculate two squared, we would type:

= 2 ^ 2

To calculate the square root of two, we need to calculate 2 to the power of one half:

= 2 ^ (1/2)

Any calculation in brackets is done first. If this is going past what you remember of school maths, don't panic. I have given detailed instructions for everything you need to create the spreadsheet.

Experiment a bit if you have never used a spreadsheet before. Spreadsheets are easy when you get the hang of them, and you can do almost anything with them. Your program should have a tutorial or an introductory information page to help you get started.

The mortgage spreadsheet

Here is the spreadsheet calculation for mortgage payments and a similar calculation done on a calculator. Set this up for the values I have used first, so you can see that you have got it right, then substitute the values for your own loan.

You may like to set up a worksheet for your original loan, or for the amount you currently owe, for the standard payment amount. Print this if you are working on a computer, and file it away so you can compare where you are as you pay your loan off faster.

Once you have set this up, you can change the payments to see what happens if you pay more into your loan. To judge the effect of having an offset account, work out the interest on the average balance at the home loan rate, divide this by the number of payments in the year, and add this value to the payment.

You can recalculate your worksheet each year when you

get your new statement from your bank. I will give you some ideas for this in the next section.

The spreadsheet

First set up the top part of the worksheet with the **Principal** in E3, the **Interest rate** in E4, the total **Number of Payments** (months) for your loan in E5, the actual **Payment** you will be making per month in E6 and the **Minimum** you are obliged to pay in E7.

The interest rate can be put in as a fraction, e.g. 0.07 for 7 per cent, or you can type in 7% if you want to, and Excel will convert it to a fraction for you.

If you are paying off your mortgage fortnightly, you can set up your spreadsheet for fortnightly payments, however this will give you a very long worksheet. You can work on a monthly worksheet, by multiplying the fortnightly payment by 2.17. This will be accurate to within a few dollars.

If you are already paying a loan off, look back to your last statement to see how much you owed at the beginning of this year and use that for the Principal. Or phone your bank for a more accurate current amount. Use the number of payments you still have to make, and your own interest rate.

To work out the standard monthly amount you need to pay, the formula is:

$$\text{Payment} = \frac{P \times r \times (1 + r)^n}{(1 + r)^n - 1}$$

P is the Principal.

r is the interest rate per period, in this case the yearly rate divided by 12

n is the number of payments. For a 25-year loan, this would be 300.

The computer can calculate this for you once you have put in the Principal, the Interest Rate and the number of Payments. The formula in cell E7 is:

=(E3*E4/12*(1+E4/12)^E5)/((1+E4/12)^E5-1)

Or you can use the Excel payment function =PMT, to work this out. The format for this is:

=PMT(Interest rate per mth, No. of mths,–present value, future value, type)

The present value is the amount you owe. You will need to put a minus in front of this amount. The future value is zero because you will have paid the loan off. The type is zero because the payment is made at the end of each month. The function looks like this:

=PMT(E4/12,E5,-E3,0,0)

Put the payment you are actually making per month in E6. This is the minimum payment, plus any extra you are putting in, plus the interest gain on any amount in an offset account. This offset is interest you are saving, so effectively it is money you are paying off your loan, and is part of your monthly payment. Estimate your average offset account balance then multiply this by the offset rate and divide by 12 to give the value for one month.

Set up the headings in Row 9. You will need **Year, Payment No, Owing, Principal, Interest, Total Paid, Total Interest** and **Now Owing.**

Format the cells for all columns from here on as whole dollars. This makes it much easier to read. We are not accurate to closer than this anyway, because we are ignoring fees. Select the next 300 rows, choose **Format → Cells → Number**, and select how many decimal places you want, in this case zero.

In the **Year** column, you will need to put each year number from 1 to 25 in twelve times. This is only used to keep track of where you are as you look down the worksheet, so you can see at a glance how many years it will take to pay out the loan. To do this, put 1 in cells A10 to A21, then set cell A22 to:

=A10 + 1

Now copy cell A22 to cells A23 to A310. If your loan is for more than 25 years, just continue down for as many years you need.

For **Payment No**, you need 1 to 300 as you go down the column. Just set the first line to 1, and the other lines to the previous cell plus one, so B11 is:

=B10 + 1

Then just copy this down the page. If your standard loan is less than or more than 25 years, go down to the number of months for your loan.

The **Amount Owing** is the Principal at the beginning of the month. For the first row, set this equal to the Principal in E3. For subsequent rows, set it equal to the Now Owing for the end of the previous month from column H. So cell C11 will be:

=H10

Now copy cell C11 to the rest of this column.

The **Principal** is the portion of that month's payment representing the Principal repayment. This is the payment we are making (in E6), less the interest amount that we are about to calculate in the next column.

This will give cell D10 as:

=$E$6 – E10

The **Interest** is the portion of that month's payment representing the Interest for that month. To calculate this, just divide the interest rate by 12, and multiply this by the amount owing at the beginning of the month. This gives for E10:

=C10 * $E$4/12

The **Total Paid** is the total amount you have paid into your loan from the first payment. This is the sum of the principal and interest columns from the beginning to the row you are on. Cell F10 will be:

=SUM($D$10:D10,$E$10:E10)

Just copy this to the rest of the column and the cell references will update automatically.

The **Total Interest** is the interest you have paid from the first payment. This is calculated in the same way, but just sum the interest in column E. So G10 is:

=SUM($E$10:E10)

The **Now Owing** column is just the original principal, less the principal we have paid off the loan this month. Set H10 to:

=C10 – D10

Copy these calculations from this row for columns D to H to the rest of each column.

Table S.1 shows the spreadsheet for the minimum payment.

If you are working this out on the minimum payment, your spreadsheet should reduce to zero at the end of year 25. If you are paying extra, it will reduce to zero much sooner and you will have a lot of negative numbers in the last years. The pay-off times and amounts are for the month where the values reach zero or first become slightly negative. If you format the cells with negative numbers in red, it will be easier to see where you pay the loan off.

If you want to keep the spreadsheet separately, copy it to a new sheet, delete all the negative lines after the payout month, and adjust the last payment so you end up with zero.

Table 7.1 Mortgage Spreadsheet

PRINCIPAL	100 000
INTEREST RATE	7%
NUMBER OF PAYMENTS	300
PAYMENT	706.78
MINIMUM PAYMENT	706.78

YR	PMT	OWING	PRINC	INTEREST	TOT PAID	TOT INT	NOW OWE
1	1	100 000	123	583	707	583	99 877
1	2	99 877	124	583	1 414	1 166	99 752
1	3	99 752	125	582	2 120	1 748	99 627
1	4	99 627	126	581	2 827	2 329	99 502
1	5	99 502	126	580	3 534	2 909	99 376
1	6	99 376	127	580	4 241	3 489	99 248
.	.	.	.	.	.	.	.
.	.	.	.	.	.	.	.
.	.	.	.	.	.	.	.
25	295	4 155	683	24	208 500	111 973	3 473
25	296	3 473	687	20	209 207	111 993	2 786
25	297	2 786	691	16	209 913	112 009	2 096
25	298	2 096	695	12	210 620	112 021	1 401
25	299	1 401	699	8	211 327	112 030	703
25	300	703	703	4	212 034	112 034	0

To do this, put the value from the Amount Owing column (column C) in the Principal Paid (column D) for that row. The interest will work out automatically and the totals will update correctly.

If you are a spreadsheet expert, you can set your calculations up with =IF functions to check when the cells go negative and put zeros or spaces from then on.

You can also set up a smaller worksheet with a summary of the values at the end of each year. The tables in the back of this book are set up as a summary for each year. If you are new to spreadsheets, this extra table is optional.

Set the table up further across the page, from column K on, or set up a new page in your workbook. Use the same headings except for the payment number. The year is in column A. Set K11 as:

=A11

Use the Owing amount for the beginning of the year, which is in C11. Just select the cell where you want the value to go, type in = then select the cell you want to copy, in this case C1 on the original page. This is called linking cells. The principal paid for the year is the sum of the principal you paid for each month of the year. Set this to:

=SUM(D11:D22)

Calculate the interest paid for the year in the same way:

=SUM(E11:E22)

For the principal to date and the interest to date, use the values for the last row for the year, Row 22 for the first year. The Now Owing value also comes from this row.

Set up the second year summary in a similar way, using the values for year two, in rows 23 to 34.

For the final year, use the values for the row where your mortgage is paid off, rather than the values for the end of that year.

Manual calculation

To work all this out on a calculator, we will need to approximate a bit so we are not working out 300 different lines. Enthusiasm would run out well before you managed a third of that! Instead of working it out monthly, we will work it out yearly. Rule up a sheet just like the computer sheet, but leave out the Payment No column, and just put 1 to 25 (or the number of years for your loan) in the year column. Add an extra year, because when we get down that far, error starts to creep in, and we may go over a bit.

Write in your Principal and Interest rate as we did for the computer worksheet.

Now look back at how we calculated the minimum payment. You can work this out on a scientific calculator, but not on a normal one. If the maths for this looks beyond your capabilities, don't panic. We don't really need to calculate this anyway. Most bank people don't even know this formula, they just look up a table or get a figure from their computer. If you have a normal calculator, you will have to get this figure from your bank, or use the repayment table in the Tables section of this book. You will know this amount anyway if you currently have a loan.

Add to the minimum payment any extra payments you are making, and the interest gain on the average amount in any offset accounts. If you are paying fortnightly, multiply your usual fortnightly payment by 2.17 to give your monthly payment.

Now work out your total annual payment by multiplying your monthly payment by 12. Round this up to the next $50 to help allow for the error in the interest calculation. Write this down as the **Payment**.

Write your Principal in the **Owing** column in the first row of the table.

Calculate the interest for the first year by multiplying the original principal by the interest rate. Put this in the **Interest** column. Don't worry that this will be slightly more than you will actually be paying, because each month you pay a little off the Principal. The only easy way to be more accurate than this is to calculate the whole three hundred lines.

Subtract the interest paid for the year from the Payment. This is the principal we have paid off the loan. Write this figure in the **Principal** column for the first row.

The **Total Paid** is the sum of all the payments to date. For the first line this will only be one payment. The **Total Interest** is $7000 for this line. The **Now Owing** column is the Original Principal ($100 000) less the Principal paid this year, which is $1500. Calculate this figure, and then transfer it to the Owing column on the next row.

Work out the Interest for the next row by multiplying the new Owing by the Interest Rate. Subtract this from the payment to give the Principal paid this year. Calculate the Total Paid to date and the Total Interest to date, and calculate the new Owing amount by subtracting the Principal paid this year from the amount Owing at the start of the year.

Continue down the rows doing the same calculation for each year.

When you reach the last amount, you may not be paying the whole year's payment, because you don't owe that much. Just adjust the principal paid to equal the final year's amount, calculate the interest, and add these figures to the totals.

You will find that when you reach year 25, you are around $5000 out. This is because we are not allowing for the interest saved as the principal is reduced during each year. Don't worry about the discrepancy. If you put your own figures into this calculation, you will get your new mortgage payout time to within a year and this is quite sufficient for our purposes.

Table 7.2 Mortgage spreadsheet manual calculation

PRINCIPAL	100 000
INTEREST RATE	7%
PAYMENT	8500

YEAR	OWING	PRINC	INTEREST	TOT PAID	TOTAL INT	NOW OWE
1	100 000	1500	7000	8 500	7 000	98 500
2	98 500	1605	6895	17 000	13 895	96 895
3	96 895	1717	6783	25 500	20 678	95 178
4	95 178	1838	6662	34 000	27 340	93 340
5	93 340	1966	6534	42 500	33 874	91 374
6	91 374	2104	6396	51 000	40 270	89 270
7	89 270	2251	6249	59 500	46 519	87 019
8	87 019	2409	6091	68 000	52 610	84 610
9	84 610	2577	5923	76 500	58 533	82 033
10	82 033	2758	5742	85 000	64 275	79 275
11	79 275	2951	5549	93 500	69 825	76 325
12	76 325	3157	5343	102 000	75 167	73 167
13	73 167	3378	5122	110 500	80 289	69 789
14	69 789	3615	4885	119 000	85 174	66 174
15	66 174	3868	4632	127 500	89 806	62 306
16	62 306	4139	4361	136 000	94 168	58 168
17	58 168	4428	4072	144 500	98 240	53 740
18	53 740	4738	3762	153 000	102 001	49 001
19	49 001	5070	3430	161 500	105 432	43 932
20	43 932	5425	3075	170 000	108 507	38 507
21	38 507	5805	2695	178 500	111 202	32 702
22	32 702	6211	2289	187 000	113 491	26 491
23	26 491	6646	1854	195 500	115 346	19 846
24	19 846	7111	1389	204 000	116 735	12 735
25	12 735	7609	891	212 500	117 626	5 126
26	5 126	5126	359	217 985	117 985	0

Recalculate this using the amount you actually owe from your home loan statement each year. When you have only three or four years to go, this method is not all that accurate, so you may want to recalculate it on a monthly basis at this stage. The monthly calculation will be reasonably accurate because the bank calculates it this way.

Here is the same worksheet recalculated with a payment of $1000 per month, which is around $300 per month more than the minimum, in extra payments and offset. You can see from this the dramatic interest saving over the life of the loan of around $60 000. Remember the manual calculation is accurate only to a few thousand dollars.

Table 7.3 Mortgage worksheet with extra payment

PRINCIPAL	100 000
INTEREST RATE	7%
PAYMENT	12 000

YEAR	OWING	PRINC	INTEREST	TOT PAID	TOTAL INT	NOW OWE
1	100 000	5 000	7000	12 000	7 000	95 000
2	95 000	5 350	6650	24 000	13 650	89 650
3	89 650	5 725	6276	36 000	19 926	83 926
4	83 926	6 125	5875	48 000	25 800	77 800
5	77 800	6 554	5446	60 000	31 246	71 246
6	71 246	7 013	4987	72 000	36 234	64 234
7	64 234	7 504	4496	84 000	40 730	56 730
8	56 730	8 029	3971	96 000	44 701	48 701
9	48 701	8 591	3409	108 000	48 110	40 110
10	40 110	9 192	2808	120 000	50 918	30 918
11	30 918	9 836	2164	132 000	53 082	21 082
12	21 082	10 524	1476	144 000	54 558	10 558
13	10 558	10 558	739	155 297	55 297	0

Using your spreadsheet

Once you have set up a mortgage spreadsheet, you can use it to track where you are on a payment-by-payment basis. Set up two identical worksheets on your spreadsheet and name them **Original** and **Current.** To copy a worksheet select **Edit → Move or Copy Sheet**, then check the box that says **Create a Copy** and choose where you want to locate the sheet.

Original worksheet

For the original worksheet, you only need to change the values when the mortgage rate changes. You cannot simply change the rate at the top of the page, however, as the payments to date were at the old mortgage rate.

What you need to do is lock in the actual values of the payments you have already made, then recalculate the values for future payments. Select the rows for the payments you have already made, select **Edit → Copy**, then **Edit → Paste Special → Values.**

This will convert all the formulae to amounts. You can then change the mortgage rate at the top of the page, and the remaining lines will calculate at the new rate.

The rate may have changed partway through a payment. Don't worry about this. Just convert the values up to the closest payment to the rate change. You will be accurate within a few dollars.

Current worksheet

For the second worksheet, you can keep track of the payments you actually make. It will make it easier if you put in the year and month for your payments in Column I, so you know where you are.

To do this, first put the date you made your first mortgage payment in Column I on the first row of the spreadsheet (Row 11 if you set it up as instructed). Now select the cells in Column I from the date down to the last worksheet row. Select **Edit → Fill → Series → Column → Date → Month** and set **Step Value** to 1. This should fill in the column for you with the payment date corresponding to that row.

Put your actual payment you made for the month in the Payment cell at the top of your worksheet. Now select the row for the month you made the payment, and select **Edit → Copy**, then **Edit → Paste Special** and select **Values**.

If the payment you made was different to the payment you normally make, just change the payment back to your normal value before saving the worksheet. Update the payment each month in this way, and you will have a good indication of where you are and what you still owe. You can compare this to the original loan worksheet to see how well you are going.

If some of your payment is in offset, then you will need to wait until you get a loan statement to know the total value of your payment for the month. Check that your outstanding loan balance agrees with the statement and, if not, adjust the balance on your worksheet by putting this value into the Owing column (Column C) on your worksheet for the next row.

You will be able to keep a reasonable estimate of where you are, how much you still owe, when you are likely to have paid off your loan, and how much interest you will be saving overall by keeping track of your payments in this way.

Equations and functions

Here is a summary of all equations and functions used in the spreadsheets.

Repayment amount

To work out the standard monthly amount you need to pay, the formula is:

$$\text{Payment} = \frac{P \times r \times (1 + r)^n}{(1 + r)^n - 1}$$

P is the Principal.

r is the interest rate per period, in this case the yearly rate divided by 12

n is the number of payments. For a 25 year loan, this would be 300.

The function for Excel is:

=PMT(Interest rate per mth, No of mths,–present value, future value, type)

The present value is the amount you owe. The future value is zero because you will have paid the loan off. The type is zero because the payment is made at the end of each month.

Number of payments

This formula gives the number of payments you will make to pay off a given principal amount with a set payment amount:

$$n = \frac{\ln (a / (a - P \times r))}{\ln (1 + r)}$$

n is the number of payments

a is the payment amount

P is the principal
r is the interest rate per period
ln is the natural log function

The corresponding Excel formula is:
=NPER(interest rate, payment amount, present value, future value, type)

Future value of an investment

The formula for the future value of an investment is:

Future Value = $P \times (1 + r)^n$

P is the amount invested
r is the interest rate per period
n is the number of periods

This, however, only gives you a value for a single amount you invest. In our investment return table we are adding another $1000 each month. The future value of the following month's payment would be the same calculation for one less month. You could in theory calculate this for each monthly investment, then add them together. However, this is a time-consuming calculation to do with a calculator.

The spreadsheet formula for future value does cover the situation where you are adding to your investment at a constant rate. The formula for Excel is:

=FV(rate per period, no of periods,–payment per period,–starting value, type)

You will need to divide the annual rate by 12 as you are working in months. The starting value is zero, as we are starting with nothing, and the type is 1, because we are adding our payment at the beginning of the month.

Tables

Repayment amounts for 25-year loan

Table A gives the minimum per month payment for a 25-year mortgage of $100 000 for various interest rates. If your interest rate falls between two percentages, make an estimate between the two.

Adjust for your loan amount by simple scaling, for example, if your loan is for $150 000, your payment will be 1.5 times the payment for $100 000. If your interest rate falls between values and you want an accurate repayment amount, the formula was given previously in the Equations and Functions section (see p 232).

Table 8.1 Repayment amounts for $100 000 over 25 years for various interest rates

Rate	Payment	Rate	Payment	Rate	Payment
4.00	527.84	7.00	706.78	10.00	908.70
4.25	541.74	7.25	722.81	10.25	926.38
4.50	555.83	7.50	738.99	10.50	944.18
4.75	570.12	7.75	755.33	10.75	962.09
5.00	584.59	8.00	771.82	11.00	980.11
5.25	599.25	8.25	788.45	11.25	998.24
5.50	614.09	8.50	805.23	11.50	1016.47
5.75	629.11	8.75	822.14	11.75	1034.80
6.00	644.30	9.00	839.20	12.00	1053.22
6.25	659.67	9.25	856.38	12.25	1071.74
6.50	675.21	9.50	873.70	12.50	1090.35
6.75	690.91	9.75	891.14	12.75	1109.05
7.00	706.78	10.00	908.70	13.00	1127.84
7.25	722.81	10.25	926.38	13.25	1146.70
7.50	738.99	10.50	944.18	13.50	1165.64
7.75	755.33	10.75	962.09	13.75	1184.67
8.00	771.82	11.00	980.11	14.00	1203.76
8.25	788.45	11.25	998.24	14.25	1222.93
8.50	805.23	11.50	1016.47	14.50	1242.16
8.75	822.14	11.75	1034.80	14.75	1261.46
9.00	839.20	12.00	1053.22	15.00	1280.83

Mortgage tables

The following pages give tables of mortgage repayments for a loan of $100 000 for range of interest rates from 5 per cent to 9 per cent for a 25-year term. The first table for each interest rate gives the standard worksheet for paying off the loan in the normal way. The second table gives the monthly payment amount required to pay off the loan in a set number of years from 1 to 30. The final table for each interest rate gives the time and interest you will save for a range of extra payments.

If your mortgage is for a different amount, you can calculate the values for your loan by proportioning the value. For example, if your loan is for $150 000, you can multiply all values by 1.5.

If your rate is between two tables, just choose the closest rate. Mortgage rates can vary over time and the extra amount you have available to add to your payment will vary over time. The calculations are meant as a guide to what can be achieved, not to calculate your loan to the nearest dollar.

You can use the monthly payment tables to work out how much you need to pay if you want to pay off your loan off over a set number of years. Remember to proportion the figures for the amount of your loan (for example, multiply by 1.5 for a $150 000 loan).

The table of extra payments will give you some idea of the time and interest you will save for a given amount extra paid each month. If you pay your mortgage fortnightly, divide this extra amount by 2.17. For weekly, divide by 4.33. Again, adjust for your loan amount.

These tables are available for a wider range of interest rates from my website. See the Useful Websites section for the address.

Table 8.2 Worksheet for a standard $100 000 mortgage paid off over 25 years at 5.0%

PRINCIPAL	100 000
INTEREST RATE	5.0%
NO OF PAYMENTS	300
PAYMENT	584.59
MIN PAYMENT	584.59

YR	OWING	PRINC	INTEREST	TOT PAID	TOT INT	NOW OWE
1	100 000	2062	4953	7 015	4 953	97 938
2	97 938	2167	4848	14 030	9 801	95 771
3	95 771	2278	4737	21 045	14 538	93 492
4	93 492	2395	4620	28 060	19 158	91 098
5	91 098	2517	4498	35 075	23 656	88 580
6	88 580	2646	4369	42 090	28 025	85 934
7	85 934	2782	4234	49 106	32 258	83 152
8	83 152	2924	4091	56 121	36 349	80 229
9	80 229	3073	3942	63 136	40 291	77 155
10	77 155	3231	3784	70 151	44 075	73 924
11	73 924	3396	3619	77 166	47 694	70 528
12	70 528	3570	3445	84 181	51 140	66 959
13	66 959	3752	3263	91 196	54 402	63 206
14	63 206	3944	3071	98 211	57 473	59 262
15	59 262	4146	2869	105 226	60 342	55 116
16	55 116	4358	2657	112 241	62 999	50 758
17	50 758	4581	2434	119 256	65 433	46 176
18	46 176	4816	2199	126 271	67 632	41 361
19	41 361	5062	1953	133 287	69 585	36 299
20	36 299	5321	1694	140 302	71 279	30 978
21	30 978	5593	1422	147 317	72 701	25 385
22	25 385	5879	1136	154 332	73 837	19 505
23	19 505	6180	835	161 347	74 672	13 325
24	13 325	6496	519	168 362	75 191	6 829
25	6 829	6829	186	175 377	75 377	0

Table 8.3 Monthly payment amounts for $100 000 for 1 to 30 years at 5.0%

Years	Per month	Years	Per month	Years	Per month
1	8561	11	986	21	642
2	4387	12	925	22	625
3	2997	13	873	23	610
4	2303	14	829	24	597
5	1887	15	791	25	585
6	1610	16	758	26	573
7	1413	17	729	27	563
8	1266	18	703	28	554
9	1152	19	680	29	545
10	1061	20	660	30	537

Table 8.4 Value of extra payments for $100 000 loan at 5.0%

BASE PAYMENT	585
ORIGINAL TOTAL	175 377
ORIGINAL INTEREST	75 377

Extra payment $	Years to pay	Years saved	Amount saved $
0	25.0	0.0	0
10	24.2	0.8	2 846
20	23.4	1.6	5 470
50	21.4	3.6	12 253
100	18.8	6.2	20 922
150	16.8	8.2	27 417
200	15.2	9.8	32 482
250	13.9	11.1	36 551
300	12.8	12.2	39 898
400	11.0	14.0	45 084
500	9.7	15.3	48 924
600	8.7	16.3	51 886
700	7.9	17.1	54 243
800	7.2	17.8	56 163
900	6.6	18.4	57 759
1000	6.1	18.9	59 106

Table 8.5 Worksheet for a standard $100 000 mortgage paid off over 25 years at 5.5%

PRINCIPAL	100 000
INTEREST RATE	5.5%
NO OF PAYMENTS	300
PAYMENT	614.09
MIN PAYMENT	614.09

YR	OWING	PRINC	INTEREST	TOT PAID	TOT INT	NOW OWE
1	100 000	1917	5452	7 369	5 452	98 083
2	98 083	2025	5344	14 738	10 796	96 058
3	96 058	2139	5230	22 107	16 026	93 919
4	93 919	2260	5109	29 476	21 135	91 659
5	91 659	2387	4982	36 845	26 117	89 272
6	89 272	2522	4847	44 214	30 964	86 749
7	86 749	2664	4705	51 583	35 668	84 085
8	84 085	2815	4554	58 952	40 223	81 271
9	81 271	2973	4396	66 321	44 619	78 297
10	78 297	3141	4228	73 690	48 847	75 156
11	75 156	3318	4051	81 060	52 897	71 838
12	71 838	3505	3864	88 429	56 761	68 332
13	68 332	3703	3666	95 798	60 427	64 629
14	64 629	3912	3457	103 167	63 884	60 717
15	60 717	4133	3236	110 536	67 120	56 584
16	56 584	4366	3003	117 905	70 123	52 218
17	52 218	4612	2757	125 274	72 880	47 606
18	47 606	4872	2497	132 643	75 377	42 734
19	42 734	5147	2222	140 012	77 599	37 587
20	37 587	5437	1932	147 381	79 530	32 149
21	32 149	5744	1625	154 750	81 155	26 405
22	26 405	6068	1301	162 119	82 456	20 337
23	20 337	6411	959	169 488	83 414	13 926
24	13 926	6772	597	176 857	84 011	7 154
25	7 154	7154	215	184 226	84 226	0

Table 8.6 Monthly payment amounts for $100 000 for 1 to 30 years at 5.5%

Years	Per month	Years	Per month	Years	Per month
1	8584	11	1011	21	670
2	4410	12	950	22	654
3	3020	13	899	23	639
4	2326	14	855	24	626
5	1910	15	817	25	614
6	1634	16	784	26	603
7	1437	17	756	27	593
8	1290	18	730	28	584
9	1176	19	708	29	576
10	1085	20	688	30	568

Table 8.7 Value of extra payments for $100 000 loan at 5.5%

BASE PAYMENT	614
ORIGINAL TOTAL	184 226
ORIGINAL INTEREST	84 226

Extra payment $	Years to pay	Years saved	Amount saved $
0	25.0	0.0	0
10	24.2	0.8	3 288
20	23.4	1.6	6 307
50	21.4	3.6	14 063
100	18.7	6.3	23 885
150	16.7	8.3	31 187
200	15.1	9.9	36 852
250	13.8	11.2	41 386
300	12.7	12.3	45 105
400	11.0	14.0	50 854
500	9.7	15.3	55 101
600	8.6	16.4	58 372
700	7.8	17.2	60 971
800	7.1	17.9	63 087
900	6.6	18.4	64 845
1000	6.1	18.9	66 328

Table 8.8 Worksheet for a standard $100 000 mortgage paid off over 25 years at 6.0%

PRINCIPAL	100 000
INTEREST RATE	6.0%
NO OF PAYMENTS	300
PAYMENT	644.30
MIN PAYMENT	644.30

YR	OWING	PRINC	INTEREST	TOT PAID	TOT INT	NOW OWE
1	100 000	1780	5952	7 732	5 952	98 220
2	98 220	1890	5842	15 463	11 793	96 330
3	96 330	2006	5725	23 195	17 519	94 324
4	94 324	2130	5601	30 926	23 120	92 194
5	92 194	2262	5470	38 658	28 590	89 932
6	89 932	2401	5331	46 390	33 921	87 531
7	87 531	2549	5183	54 121	39 103	84 982
8	84 982	2706	5025	61 853	44 129	82 276
9	82 276	2873	4858	69 585	48 987	79 402
10	79 402	3050	4681	77 316	53 668	76 352
11	76 352	3239	4493	85 048	58 161	73 113
12	73 113	3438	4293	92 779	62 454	69 675
13	69 675	3650	4081	100 511	66 536	66 025
14	66 025	3876	3856	108 243	70 392	62 149
15	62 149	4115	3617	115 974	74 009	58 034
16	58 034	4368	3363	123 706	77 372	53 666
17	53 666	4638	3094	131 437	80 466	49 028
18	49 028	4924	2808	139 169	83 273	44 104
19	44 104	5228	2504	146 901	85 778	38 877
20	38 877	5550	2182	154 632	87 959	33 327
21	33 327	5892	1839	162 364	89 799	27 435
22	27 435	6256	1476	170 096	91 274	21 179
23	21 179	6642	1090	177 827	92 364	14 537
24	14 537	7051	680	185 559	93 045	7 486
25	7 486	7486	246	193 290	93 290	0

Table 8.9 Monthly payment amounts for $100 000 for 1 to 30 years at 6.0%

Years	Per month	Years	Per month	Years	Per month
1	8607	11	1037	21	699
2	4432	12	976	22	683
3	3042	13	925	23	669
4	2349	14	881	24	656
5	1933	15	844	25	644
6	1657	16	811	26	634
7	1461	17	783	27	624
8	1314	18	758	28	615
9	1201	19	736	29	607
10	1110	20	716	30	600

Table 8.10 Value of Extra Payments for $100 000 loan at 6.0%

BASE PAYMENT	644
ORIGINAL TOTAL	193 290
ORIGINAL INTEREST	93 290

Extra payment $	Years to pay	Years saved	Amount saved $
0	25.0	0.0	0
10	24.1	0.9	3 770
20	23.3	1.7	7 217
50	21.3	3.7	16 011
100	18.6	6.4	27 039
150	16.6	8.4	35 171
200	15.0	10.0	41 446
250	13.7	11.3	46 451
300	12.6	12.4	50 545
400	10.9	14.1	56 857
500	9.6	15.4	61 509
600	8.6	16.4	65 086
700	7.8	17.2	67 926
800	7.1	17.9	70 237
900	6.5	18.5	72 155
1000	6.1	18.9	73 774

Table 8.11 Worksheet for a standard $100 000 mortgage paid off over 25 years at 6.5%

PRINCIPAL	100 000
INTEREST RATE	6.5%
NO OF PAYMENTS	300
PAYMENT	675.21
MIN PAYMENT	675.21

YR	OWING	PRINC	INTEREST	TOT PAID	TOT INT	NOW OWE
1	100 000	1651	6451	8 102	6 451	98 349
2	98 349	1762	6341	16 205	12 792	96 587
3	96 587	1880	6223	24 307	19 015	94 708
4	94 708	2006	6097	32 410	25 112	92 702
5	92 702	2140	5963	40 512	31 075	90 562
6	90 562	2283	5819	48 615	36 894	88 279
7	88 279	2436	5666	56 717	42 560	85 843
8	85 843	2599	5503	64 820	48 064	83 244
9	83 244	2773	5329	72 922	53 393	80 470
10	80 470	2959	5143	81 025	58 536	77 511
11	77 511	3157	4945	89 127	63 481	74 354
12	74 354	3369	4734	97 230	68 215	70 986
13	70 986	3594	4508	105 332	72 724	67 391
14	67 391	3835	4268	113 435	76 991	63 556
15	63 556	4092	4011	121 537	81 002	59 464
16	59 464	4366	3737	129 640	84 738	55 099
17	55 099	4658	3444	137 742	88 183	50 440
18	50 440	4970	3132	145 845	91 315	45 470
19	45 470	5303	2799	153 947	94 114	40 167
20	40 167	5658	2444	162 050	96 559	34 509
21	34 509	6037	2065	170 152	98 624	28 472
22	28 472	6441	1661	178 255	100 285	22 030
23	22 030	6873	1230	186 357	101 515	15 157
24	15 157	7333	769	194 460	102 284	7 824
25	7 824	7824	278	202 562	102 562	0

Table 8.12 Monthly payment amounts for $100 000 for 1 to 30 years at 6.5%

Years	Per month	Years	Per month	Years	Per month
1	8630	11	1062	21	728
2	4455	12	1002	22	713
3	3065	13	951	23	699
4	2371	14	908	24	687
5	1957	15	871	25	675
6	1681	16	839	26	665
7	1485	17	811	27	656
8	1339	18	787	28	647
9	1225	19	765	29	639
10	1135	20	746	30	632

Table 8.13 Value of extra payments for $100 000 loan at 6.5%

BASE PAYMENT	675
ORIGINAL TOTAL	202 562
ORIGINAL INTEREST	102 562

Extra payment $	Years to pay	Years saved	Amount saved $
0	25.0	0.0	0
10	24.1	0.9	4 295
20	23.3	1.7	8 204
50	21.2	3.8	18 104
100	18.5	6.5	30 392
150	16.5	8.5	39 374
200	14.9	10.1	46 268
250	13.6	11.4	51 747
300	12.5	12.5	56 217
400	10.8	14.2	63 090
500	9.5	15.5	68 144
600	8.5	16.5	72 025
700	7.7	17.3	75 104
800	7.1	17.9	77 608
900	6.5	18.5	79 685
1000	6.0	19.0	81 438

Table 8.14 Worksheet for a standard $100 000 mortgage paid off over 25 years at 7.0%

PRINCIPAL	100 000
INTEREST RATE	7.0%
NO OF PAYMENTS	300
PAYMENT	706.28
MIN PAYMENT	706.28

YR	OWING	PRINC	INTEREST	TOT PAID	TOT INT	NOW OWE
1	100 000	1530	6952	8 481	6 952	98 470
2	98 470	1640	6841	16 963	13 792	96 830
3	96 830	1759	6722	25 444	20 515	95 071
4	95 071	1886	6595	33 925	27 110	93 185
5	93 185	2022	6459	42 407	33 569	91 162
6	91 162	2169	6313	50 888	39 882	88 993
7	88 993	2325	6156	59 369	46 037	86 668
8	86 668	2494	5988	67 851	52 025	84 174
9	84 174	2674	5808	76 332	57 833	81 501
10	81 501	2867	5614	84 814	63 447	78 633
11	78 633	3074	5407	93 295	68 854	75 559
12	75 559	3297	5185	101 776	74 039	72 262
13	72 262	3535	4946	110 258	78 985	68 727
14	68 727	3791	4691	118 739	83 676	64 937
15	64 937	4065	4417	127 220	88 093	60 872
16	60 872	4358	4123	135 702	92 216	56 514
17	56 514	4673	3808	144 183	96 023	51 841
18	51 841	5011	3470	152 664	99 494	46 829
19	46 829	5374	3108	161 146	102 601	41 456
20	41 456	5762	2719	169 627	105 321	35 694
21	35 694	6179	2303	178 108	107 624	29 515
22	29 515	6625	1856	186 590	109 480	22 890
23	22 890	7104	1377	195 071	110 857	15 786
24	15 786	7618	864	203 552	111 721	8 168
25	8 168	8168	313	212 034	112 034	0

Table 8.15 Monthly payment amounts for $100 000 for 1 to 30 years at 7.0%

Years	Per month	Years	Per month	Years	Per month
1	8653	11	1088	21	758
2	4477	12	1028	22	743
3	3088	13	978	23	730
4	2395	14	935	24	718
5	1980	15	899	25	707
6	1705	16	867	26	697
7	1509	17	840	27	688
8	1363	18	816	28	680
9	1251	19	794	29	672
10	1161	20	775	30	665

Table 8.16 Value of extra payments for $100 000 loan at 7.0%

BASE PAYMENT	707
ORIGINAL TOTAL	212 034
ORIGINAL INTEREST	112 034

Extra payment $	Years to pay	Years saved	Amount saved $
0	25.0	0.0	0
10	24.1	0.9	4 868
20	23.2	1.8	9 276
50	21.1	3.9	20 353
100	18.4	6.6	33 949
150	16.4	8.6	43 801
200	14.8	10.2	51 321
250	13.5	11.5	57 275
300	12.4	12.6	62 120
400	10.7	14.3	69 552
500	9.5	15.5	75 004
600	8.5	16.5	79 186
700	7.7	17.3	82 501
800	7.0	18.0	85 195
900	6.5	18.5	87 429
1000	6.0	19.0	89 314

Table 8.17 Worksheet for a standard $100 000 mortgage paid off over 25 years at 7.5%

PRINCIPAL	100 000
INTEREST RATE	7.5%
NO OF PAYMENTS	300
PAYMENT	738.99
MIN PAYMENT	738.99

YR	OWING	PRINC	INTEREST	TOT PAID	TOT INT	NOW OWE
1	100 000	1416	7452	8 868	7 452	98 584
2	98 584	1526	7342	17 736	14 794	97 058
3	97 058	1644	7224	26 604	22 018	95 414
4	95 414	1772	7096	35 472	29 114	93 642
5	93 642	1909	6958	44 339	36 072	91 733
6	91 733	2058	6810	53 207	42 882	89 675
7	89 675	2217	6650	62 075	49 533	87 457
8	87 457	2390	6478	70 943	56 011	85 068
9	85 068	2575	6293	79 811	62 304	82 493
10	82 493	2775	6093	88 679	68 396	79 718
11	79 718	2990	5877	97 547	74 274	76 727
12	76 727	3223	5645	106 415	79 919	73 504
13	73 504	3473	5395	115 283	85 314	70 032
14	70 032	3742	5125	124 151	90 440	66 289
15	66 289	4033	4835	133 018	95 275	62 256
16	62 256	4346	4522	141 886	99 796	57 910
17	57 910	4683	4184	150 754	103 981	53 227
18	53 227	5047	3821	159 622	107 802	48 180
19	48 180	5439	3429	168 490	111 231	42 741
20	42 741	5861	3007	177 358	114 237	36 880
21	36 880	6316	2552	186 226	116 789	30 563
22	30 563	6806	2061	195 094	118 851	23 757
23	23 757	7335	1533	203 962	120 384	16 422
24	16 422	7904	964	212 829	121 347	8 518
25	8 518	8518	350	221 697	121 697	0

Table 8.18 Monthly payment amounts for $100 000 for 1 to 30 years at 7.5%

Years	Per month	Years	Per month	Years	Per month
1	8676	11	1115	21	789
2	4500	12	1055	22	775
3	3111	13	1005	23	761
4	2418	14	963	24	750
5	2004	15	927	25	739
6	1729	16	896	26	729
7	1534	17	869	27	721
8	1388	18	845	28	713
9	1276	19	824	29	706
10	1187	20	806	30	699

Table 8.19 Value of extra payments for $100 000 loan at 7.5%

BASE PAYMENT	739
ORIGINAL TOTAL	221 697
ORIGINAL INTEREST	121 697

Extra payment $	Years to pay	Years saved	Amount saved $
0	25.0	0.0	0
10	24.1	0.9	5 493
20	23.2	1.8	10 439
50	21.0	4.0	22 765
100	18.3	6.7	37 719
150	16.2	8.8	48 456
200	14.7	10.3	56 606
250	13.4	11.6	63 035
300	12.3	12.7	68 254
400	10.6	14.4	76 239
500	9.4	15.6	82 085
600	8.4	16.6	86 563
700	7.6	17.4	90 110
800	7.0	18.0	92 991
900	6.4	18.6	95 381
1000	6.0	19.0	97 395

Table 8.20 Worksheet for a standard $100 000 mortgage paid off over 25 years at 8.0%

PRINCIPAL	100 000
INTEREST RATE	8.0%
NO OF PAYMENTS	300
PAYMENT	771.82
MIN PAYMENT	771.82

YR	OWING	PRINC	INTEREST	TOT PAID	TOT INT	NOW OWE
1	100 000	1309	7953	9 262	7 953	98 691
2	98 691	1418	7844	18 524	15 797	97 273
3	97 273	1535	7726	27 785	23 523	95 738
4	95 738	1663	7599	37 047	31 122	94 075
5	94 075	1801	7461	46 309	38 583	92 274
6	92 274	1950	7311	55 571	45 894	90 324
7	90 324	2112	7150	64 833	53 044	88 211
8	88 211	2288	6974	74 094	60 018	85 924
9	85 924	2477	6784	83 356	66 803	83 446
10	83 446	2683	6579	92 618	73 381	80 763
11	80 763	2906	6356	101 880	79 737	77 858
12	77 858	3147	6115	111 142	85 852	74 711
13	74 711	3408	5854	120 403	91 706	71 303
14	71 303	3691	5571	129 665	97 277	67 612
15	67 612	3997	5264	138 927	102 541	63 614
16	63 614	4329	4933	148 189	107 474	59 285
17	59 285	4688	4573	157 451	112 047	54 597
18	54 597	5078	4184	166 712	116 231	49 519
19	49 519	5499	3763	175 974	119 994	44 020
20	44 020	5955	3306	185 236	123 301	38 065
21	38 065	6450	2812	194 498	126 113	31 615
22	31 615	6985	2277	203 759	128 390	24 630
23	24 630	7565	1697	213 021	130 087	17 065
24	17 065	8193	1069	222 283	131 156	8 873
25	8 873	8873	389	231 545	131 545	0

Table 8.21 Monthly payment amounts for $100 000 for 1 to 30 years at 8.0%

AMOUNT	100 000
RATE	8.0%

Years	Per month	Years	Per month	Years	Per month
1	8699	11	1142	21	820
2	4523	12	1082	22	806
3	3134	13	1033	23	793
4	2441	14	991	24	782
5	2028	15	956	25	772
6	1753	16	925	26	763
7	1559	17	898	27	754
8	1414	18	875	28	747
9	1302	19	855	29	740
10	1213	20	836	30	734

Table 8.22 Value of extra payments for $100 000 loan at 8.0%

BASE PAYMENT	772
ORIGINAL TOTAL	231 545
ORIGINAL INTEREST	131 545

Extra payment $	Years to pay	Years saved	Amount saved $
0	25.0	0.0	0
10	24.0	1.0	6 175
20	23.1	1.9	11 702
50	20.9	4.1	25 350
100	18.1	6.9	41 708
150	16.1	8.9	53 343
200	14.5	10.5	62 125
250	13.3	11.7	69 028
300	12.2	12.8	74 616
400	10.6	14.4	83 148
500	9.3	15.7	89 382
600	8.3	16.7	94 151
700	7.6	17.4	97 926
800	6.9	18.1	100 992
900	6.4	18.6	103 533
1000	5.9	19.1	105 676

Table 8.23 Worksheet for a standard $100,000 mortgage paid off over 25 years at 8.5%

PRINCIPAL	100 000
INTEREST RATE	8.5%
NO OF PAYMENTS	300
PAYMENT	805.23
MIN PAYMENT	805.23

YR	OWING	PRINC	INTEREST	TOT PAID	TOT INT	NOW OWE
1	100 000	1209	8454	9 663	8 454	98 791
2	98 791	1316	8347	19 325	16 800	97 475
3	97 475	1432	8230	28 988	25 031	96 043
4	96 043	1559	8104	38 651	33 135	94 484
5	94 484	1697	7966	48 314	41 101	92 787
6	92 787	1847	7816	57 976	48 917	90 940
7	90 940	2010	7653	67 639	56 569	88 930
8	88 930	2188	7475	77 302	64 045	86 743
9	86 743	2381	7282	86 965	71 326	84 362
10	84 362	2591	7071	96 627	78 398	81 771
11	81 771	2820	6842	106 290	85 240	78 950
12	78 950	3070	6593	115 953	91 833	75 880
13	75 880	3341	6322	125 615	98 155	72 539
14	72 539	3636	6026	135 278	104 181	68 903
15	68 903	3958	5705	144 941	109 886	64 945
16	64 945	4308	5355	154 604	115 241	60 638
17	60 638	4688	4974	164 266	120 215	55 949
18	55 949	5103	4560	173 929	124 775	50 846
19	50 846	5554	4109	183 592	128 884	45 292
20	45 292	6045	3618	193 255	132 502	39 248
21	39 248	6579	3084	202 917	135 586	32 669
22	32 669	7161	2502	212 580	138 088	25 508
23	25 508	7794	1869	222 243	139 957	17 715
24	17 715	8482	1180	231 905	141 138	9 232
25	9 232	9232	431	241 568	141 568	0

Table 8.24 Monthly payment amounts for $100,000 for 1 to 30 years at 8.5%

AMOUNT	100 000
RATE	8.5%

Years	Per month	Years	Per month	Years	Per month
1	8722	11	1169	21	852
2	4546	12	1110	22	838
3	3157	13	1061	23	826
4	2465	14	1020	24	815
5	2052	15	985	25	805
6	1778	16	954	26	796
7	1584	17	928	27	788
8	1439	18	905	28	781
9	1328	19	885	29	775
10	1240	20	868	30	769

Table 8.25 Value of Extra Payments for $100,000 loan at 8.5%

BASE PAYMENT	805
ORIGINAL TOTAL	241 568
ORIGINAL INTEREST	141 568

Extra payment $	Years to pay	Years saved	Amount saved $
0	25.0	0.0	0
10	24.0	1.0	6 919
20	23.1	1.9	13 071
50	20.8	4.2	28 117
100	18.0	7.0	45 922
150	16.0	9.0	58 464
200	14.4	10.6	67 878
250	13.1	11.9	75 250
300	12.1	12.9	81 205
400	10.5	14.5	90 274
500	9.2	15.8	96 889
600	8.3	16.7	101 944
700	7.5	17.5	105 943
800	6.9	18.1	109 190
900	6.3	18.7	111 881
1000	5.9	19.1	114 149

Table 8.26 Worksheet for a standard $100,000 mortgage paid off over 25 years at 9.0%

PRINCIPAL	100 000
INTEREST RATE	9.0%
NO OF PAYMENTS	300
PAYMENT	839.20
MIN PAYMENT	839.20

YR	OWING	PRINC	INTEREST	TOT PAID	TOT INT	NOW OWE
1	100 000	1116	8955	10 070	8 955	98 884
2	98 884	1220	8850	20 141	17 805	97 664
3	97 664	1335	8736	30 211	26 540	96 329
4	96 329	1460	8610	40 281	35 151	94 869
5	94 869	1597	8473	50 352	43 624	93 272
6	93 272	1747	8324	60 422	51 948	91 526
7	91 526	1911	8160	70 492	60 108	89 615
8	89 615	2090	7981	80 563	68 088	87 525
9	87 525	2286	7785	90 633	75 873	85 239
10	85 239	2500	7570	100 704	83 443	82 739
11	82 739	2735	7336	110 774	90 778	80 004
12	80 004	2991	7079	120 844	97 857	77 013
13	77 013	3272	6798	130 915	104 656	73 741
14	73 741	3579	6491	140 985	111 147	70 162
15	70 162	3915	6156	151 055	117 303	66 248
16	66 248	4282	5789	161 126	123 091	61 966
17	61 966	4684	5387	171 196	128 478	57 282
18	57 282	5123	4948	181 266	133 426	52 159
19	52 159	5603	4467	191 337	137 893	46 556
20	46 556	6129	3941	201 407	141 834	40 427
21	40 427	6704	3366	211 477	145 200	33 723
22	33 723	7333	2737	221 548	147 938	26 390
23	26 390	8021	2050	231 618	149 987	18 369
24	18 369	8773	1297	241 689	151 285	9 596
25	9 596	9596	474	251 759	151 759	0

Table 8.27 Monthly payment amounts for $100,000 for 1 to 30 years at 9.0%

AMOUNT 100 000
RATE 9.0%

Years	Per month	Years	Per month	Years	Per month
1	8745	11	1196	21	885
2	4568	12	1138	22	871
3	3180	13	1090	23	859
4	2489	14	1049	24	849
5	2076	15	1014	25	839
6	1803	16	985	26	831
7	1609	17	959	27	823
8	1465	18	936	28	816
9	1354	19	917	29	810
10	1267	20	900	30	805

Table 8.28 Value of Extra Payments for $100,000 loan at 9.0%

BASE PAYMENT 839
ORIGINAL TOTAL 251 759
ORIGINAL INTEREST 151 759

Extra payment $	Years to pay	Years saved	Amount saved $
0	25.0	0.0	0
10	23.9	1.1	7 730
20	23.0	2.0	14 555
50	20.7	4.3	31 075
100	17.9	7.1	50 365
150	15.8	9.2	63 821
200	14.3	10.7	73 864
250	13.0	12.0	81 701
300	12.0	13.0	88 016
400	10.4	14.6	97 614
500	9.2	15.8	104 601
600	8.2	16.8	109 936
700	7.5	17.5	114 154
800	6.8	18.2	117 578
900	6.3	18.7	120 415
1000	5.8	19.2	122 807

Investment return tables

These tables can be used to estimate the future value of $1000 invested per month for a given number of years. You can use these tables to estimate what your savings or superannuation are likely to be when you retire.

Choose the interest rate your savings are earning after allowing for tax. Choose the number of years until you retire from the table and write down the amount where the column and row cross. For 15 years at 7 per cent, this amount would be $318 881. Now divide this figure by 1000 on your calculator and multiply it by the amount that you are able to invest per month. We do the division first, so there is less chance of the number becoming too large to fit on the calculator.

For $1500 per month this would be

$$(318881/1000) \times 1500 = 478\,322$$

If you retire 15 years after you finish paying your mortgage, and you are currently paying $1500 per month, then investing this $1500 at 7 per cent for the 15 years will give you around $480 000 to retire on.

If you want to retire on a set amount, say $600 000, in a set number of years, say twenty, you can also use this same table to work out how much you need to be putting in now. If we use 7 per cent, we will have $523 595 per $1000 invested per month. Divide $600 000 by the $523 595 to give 1.146. So we need 1.146 lots of $1000. This gives $1146 a month that we need to save. This would be fairly easily achievable after you paid off your mortgage. This reduces to $736 per month for 25 years. Remember this was starting with no savings at all.

Table 8.29 Future Value of $1000 invested per month

Years	Cash in	4%	5%	6%	7%	8%
1	12 000	12 263	12 330	12 397	12 465	12 533
2	24 000	25 026	25 291	25 559	25 831	26 106
3	36 000	38 309	38 915	39 533	40 163	40 806
4	48 000	52 133	53 236	54 368	55 531	56 726
5	60 000	66 520	68 289	70 119	72 011	73 967
6	72 000	81 493	84 113	86 841	89 681	92 639
7	84 000	97 077	100 747	104 594	108 629	112 861
8	96 000	113 295	118 231	123 443	128 947	134 761
9	108 000	130 174	136 610	143 454	150 733	158 479
10	120 000	147 741	155 929	164 699	174 094	184 166
11	132 000	166 023	176 237	187 254	199 145	211 984
12	144 000	185 050	197 584	211 201	226 006	242 112
13	156 000	204 853	220 022	236 625	254 809	274 740
14	168 000	225 462	243 609	263 616	285 694	310 076
15	180 000	246 911	268 403	292 273	318 811	348 345
16	192 000	269 234	294 465	322 697	354 323	389 791
17	204 000	292 466	321 860	354 997	392 402	434 676
18	216 000	316 644	350 657	389 290	433 234	483 287
19	228 000	341 808	380 927	425 698	477 017	535 932
20	240 000	367 997	412 746	464 351	523 965	592 947
25	300 000	515 843	597 991	696 459	814 797	957 367
30	360 000	696 363	835 726	1 009 538	1 227 087	1 500 295
35	420 000	916 777	1 140 826	1 431 834	1 811 561	2 309 175
40	480 000	1 185 901	1 532 379	2 001 448	2 640 125	3 514 281

Table 8.30 Future value of $1000 invested per month

Years	Cash in	10%	12%	15%	20%
1	12 000	12 670	12 809	13 021	13 383
2	24 000	26 667	27 243	28 135	29 702
3	36 000	42 130	43 508	45 679	49 601
4	48 000	59 212	61 835	66 044	73 866
5	60 000	78 082	82 486	89 682	103 454
6	72 000	98 929	105 757	117 120	139 534
7	84 000	121 958	131 979	148 968	183 529
8	96 000	147 399	161 527	185 937	237 177
9	108 000	175 504	194 822	228 848	302 594
10	120 000	206 552	232 339	278 657	382 364
11	132 000	240 851	274 615	336 474	479 634
12	144 000	278 742	322 252	403 585	598 244
13	156 000	320 600	375 931	481 484	742 876
14	168 000	366 841	436 418	571 906	919 239
15	180 000	417 924	504 576	676 863	1 134 295
16	192 000	474 357	581 378	798 693	1 396 532
17	204 000	536 698	667 921	940 108	1 716 301
18	216 000	605 568	765 439	1 104 255	2 106 226
19	228 000	681 649	875 325	1 294 790	2 581 696
20	240 000	765 697	999 148	1 515 955	3 161 479
25	300 000	1 337 890	1 897 635	3 284 074	8 626 708
30	360 000	2 279 325	3 529 914	7 009 821	23 360 802
35	420 000	3 828 277	6 495 269	14 860 645	63 083 478
40	480 000	6 376 780	11 882 420	31 403 755	170 174 628

Index

Printed in Dunstable, United Kingdom

88126905R00160